The MURDER *of* GENEVA HARDMAN

and

LEXINGTON'S MOB RIOT OF 1920

The MURDER *of* GENEVA HARDMAN

and

LEXINGTON'S MOB RIOT OF 1920

PETER BRACKNEY

THE
History
PRESS

Published by The History Press
Charleston, SC
www.historypress.com

Copyright © 2020 by Peter Brackney
All rights reserved

Front cover, top: J. Winston Coleman Photo Collection, Transylvania University Library; *bottom*: Hardman/McGregor family collection.
Back cover: J. Winston Coleman Photo Collection, Transylvania University Library; *inset*: J. Winston Coleman Photo Collection, Transylvania University Library.

First published 2020

Manufactured in the United States

ISBN 9781467143967

Library of Congress Control Number: 2019951254

Notice: The information in this book is true and complete to the best of our knowledge. It is offered without guarantee on the part of the author or The History Press. The author and The History Press disclaim all liability in connection with the use of this book.

To the memory of Geneva—a child of unusual ability.
Mirthful.
Cheerful.
Winsome.
And sweet with a smiling countenance.

CONTENTS

Part One

Young Geneva and Her Family

T he U.S. Constitution mandates an "actual enumeration" of all persons in the United States; this enumeration is fundamental to our system of government and providing for the allocation of both representative democracy as well as taxation. Occurring every ten years, this head count acts as the largest peacetime mobilization effort in the United States. In 1910, the thirteenth decennial census commenced under an act of Congress.

It was under these conditions that Mr. Willoughby arrived at the Hardman family farm on Thursday, April 28, 1910. The farm was situated a few miles to the southeast of Hardinsburg, the county seat of Breckinridge County, Kentucky. Along with his commission and badge evidencing his official role on behalf of the national government, Willoughby carried with him the pages on which he would inscribe a snapshot of the lives he counted. Here, in Harned, Kentucky, Willoughby discovered a happy family. But over the next decade, multiple tragedies would forever change the nucleus of this American family.

The farm was owned by Rezin Hardman and his wife, Emma. Rezin was born in 1859 in the vicinity of the small community in northern Clark County, Kentucky, known as Wades Mill. Wades Mill was named after the man who operated the gristmill there on the bank of the Stoner Creek about seven and a half miles from Winchester, the county seat. Rezin's father, George, had crossed the mountains from Virginia before settling here.

In 1878, Rezin, eighteen, married a fifteen-year-old bride from Bourbon County, Emma Gillispie. Although the modern eye looks quite suspiciously on such an arrangement, the bride's young age was not an issue in the latter part of the nineteenth century. The couple exchanged their vows on January 3, 1878. The couple resided in the Clark County area for several years.

On January 25, 1910, Rezin Constant Hardman purchased the Breckinridge County farm on which the family was found by the census taker later that year. The purchase price of $3,500 for the 116 acres of farmland was paid in cash.

The census enumeration had an effective date of April 1, 1910. By that date, the Hardman family had already moved into their newly purchased farm. So, it was from here that they were counted.

By the time the Hardman family had moved to Breckinridge County, Rezin and Emma had been married some thirty-plus years. Together, they had eight children—all of whom were still living as of the 1910 census. For those who have studied their own genealogies, this is a joyful sign in and of itself considering the rates of infant mortality and those children lost at a young age in the late nineteenth and early twentieth centuries. According to the Centers for Disease Control, it was not uncommon for infant mortality rates to reach 30 percent at the dawn of the 1900s. Among the other families whose names appear on the same page of the 1910 census as the Hardmans, 15 percent of their children found an early grave.

For this good fortune alone, the Hardman family was most blessed. Their two oldest children, both sons, had already left home, presumably to start families of their own. The oldest, Ollie Hardman, lived in Clark County; the second eldest, Tupper, lived in Lexington. At the Hardman farm in Breckinridge County, the six youngest children resided with their parents. Listed first were two girls: Nellie, twenty-three, and Nettie, twenty. Willoughby did not record an occupation for either. Next were the two teenage boys: Clayton, seventeen, and Robert, sixteen. Clayton and Robert were both noted as being employed on the "home farm." It is worth noting that their employment appears to have resulted in their receiving compensation based on the census markings.

The employment of Clayton and Robert should not be overlooked. In the early twentieth century, child labor was still commonplace. Child labor laws and regulations from Washington had just begun to hit the books, but these provisions would generally not have impacted the employ of sixteen- and seventeen-year-old children as farmhands. On many family farms across America, teenage boys like Clayton and Robert would have often, if not

A young Geneva
Hardman.
*Hardman/McGregor
family collection.*

typically, worked without pay. That Rezin Hardman paid his two sons is an
indication of the family's financial security; perhaps it also indicated that
Rezin was supportive of the era's populist politics.

Then there was Pruitt, who was six years old. And, finally, the caboose
of the family was a baby girl: Geneva. Geneva Hardman was born on
September 2, 1909, in Clark County, Kentucky. She was the subject of
adoration by her family.

According to the deed for the farm in Breckinridge County, Rezin
Hardman had been a resident of Mt. Sterling, Kentucky. An examination
of the land records of Montgomery County, of which Mt. Sterling is the
county seat, do not reveal any mention of Rezin Hardman. Wades Mill, the
Clark County community in which Rezin was born, straddles the line of
these two counties. This geographic proximity may account for the reference

in the Breckinridge County deed, but that isn't the real mystery. Mt. Sterling is 165 miles from Hardinsburg. It is unexplained why the family moved west in early 1910. There is no clarity, either, in why they departed after a single season of farming.

A deed dated October 22, 1910, is included in the records of Breckinridge County. On this deed, however, Rezin and Emma Hardman were *selling* the farm they purchased just nine months earlier. They sold the land for the same amount for which they had purchased it, $3,500, except that they received only $1,000 cash when they left the Breckinridge County community of Harned. The balance would be paid with possession, which was anticipated by early spring.

The family quickly relocated to Lexington where their second eldest, Tupper, was a successful farmer. Tupper's landholdings would continue to grow until falling crop prices nationally led toward his own economic contraction. As for many farmers, the federal farm bill that passed Congress went into effect too late to assist Hardman. Tupper Hardman lost much of his property in 1929 on the eve of this country's Great Depression.

When his family returned to central Kentucky following their year in Breckinridge County, Tupper resided off the Tates Creek Road southeast of Lexington. It was on this road that tragedy first struck the Hardman family.

Rezin Constant Hardman suffered from epilepsy. According to his death certificate, Rezin had suffered from this condition for well over a year. (One could speculate whether the malady had caused either the family's removal to, or from, Breckinridge County.) On July 2, 1911, Rezin was in his buggy traveling along Tates Creek Road. At approximately 3:40 p.m., an epileptic seizure overcame him, and he fell from the buggy, dead. The preexisting condition of epilepsy, combined with the fall from his buggy, were noted as the primary and contributory causes of death on his death certificate. He was fifty-two years old.

At the time of her father's death, Geneva was not yet two. Her mother, Emma, was now a widow with an infant in her care. According to family lore, the Hardmans rallied together, and this precious child was the source of their continued joy. In 1913, Emma purchased forty acres on Walnut Hill Road (still in the southeastern quadrant of Fayette County). Emma sold that property on March 7, 1919. A day earlier, Tupper Hardman had purchased from the heirs of John Steele some eighty acres along the Harrodsburg and Perryville Pike in southwestern Fayette County. The land was situated between the South Elkhorn community and the Jessamine County line. Emma and her children remaining at home relocated there with her.

It was here in South Elkhorn that another census taker visited the Hardman family in the earliest days of 1920. Emma, now a fifty-eight-year-old widow, lived on the farm rented from her son with four of her children. Three sons—Clayton, twenty-eight, Robert, twenty-five, and Pruitt, sixteen—all helped on the farm. Nellie, thirty-three, remained at home, as did ten-year-old Geneva. Now forty-one, Ollie was the eldest child of Emma and Rezin Hardman. He, his wife, Kitty, and their four children lived in Winchester. Tupper Hardman, Emma's second born, from whom she rented her residence, and his wife, Nora, still lived on Tates Creek Road with their two boys, Joe, eleven, and Hugh, eight. A third daughter, Nettie, was married and living in Louisville with her husband and their two young children, Earl and Hugh.

The close-knit family now lived across three Kentucky counties. Nettie's husband, a Breckinridge County native, had swept her to Louisville. The ninety miles between Lexington and Louisville was a distance, but not one that was insurmountable for this loving family. Young Geneva, much closer in age to her nieces and nephews than to her own siblings, penned a note to her sister on January 24, 1920.

Lexington, Ky
Jan 24 1920.

Dear Net,
How are you all colds our colds is not much better.
Mama has just come from town with Clayton and Bob and Pruitt. Bob gave me some candy they were Rabbits.
I am going to school.
tell Earl and the baby I would like to see them.
What are you been doing,
We had a storm Friday and get dark as night at school and we good not see much and the trees was braking [sic] down. The big tree down in the sinkhole went down and another tree down by the gate.
tell Earl and the baby I will send them some book as soon as I can.
it is all most bedtime.
so I will close.
write soon,

from Geneva Hardman.

Lexington Ky
Jan 2 1920

Dear net,
How are you all colds. our colds is not
much better.
mama has just come from town
with Clayton and Bob and Prewitt.
Bob gave me som candy they were
Rabbits.
I am going to School
tell Earl and the baby I would like
to see them.
What are you been doing,
we had a strom friday and get dark
as night at School and we good not
much and the trees was brakeing
down the big tree down in sinkhole
went down and another tree down
by the gate.

2

tell Earl and the baby I will send
them some book as soon as I can
it is all most bed time.
so I will close.
write soon.
from Geneva Hardman

Handwritten letter from Geneva Hardman to her sister Nettie, written eleven days before the former's murder. *Hardman/McGregor family collection.*

The sweet note written by a ten-year-old girl speaks to her innocence. It also reminds us today of a seeming innocence of an era when handwritten notes about candy rabbits and going to school were a family's primary means of long-distance communication; an era before text messaging and social media. In fact, anyone who made Geneva's acquaintance was left with positive thoughts of the young child. Her classmates and teacher wrote that she was "cheerful, winsome, and sweet with a smiling countenance."

But the storm clouds that blotted out the sun the day before Geneva put pencil to paper were not the only storms that would wreak havoc on the South Elkhorn community that winter. Just eleven days after Geneva wrote to her sister Nettie, her life would come to a tragic end.

Part Two

A CRIME COMMITTED

OFF TO SCHOOL

"I am going to school" were a few of the words written by Geneva Hardman to her sister just eleven days earlier. And so she did.

About 7:30 a.m. on the morning of February 4, 1920, Geneva departed for the schoolhouse. The distance was about four-tenths of a mile from her home. On most mornings, a neighbor boy about Geneva's age joined her for the almost half-mile walk to school. But on February 4, he was kept at home to help on his family's farm. Severe weather, as observed in Geneva's letter to her sister, continued in late January and the first days of February; it is likely that Geneva's young walking companion was needed on the farm to help clean up from the most recent rounds of bad weather. And, so, Geneva walked alone.

The young girl, known for her sweet disposition and for being a quick study, darted between the raindrops on the cold, rainy morning. J. Winston Coleman began his pamphlet *Death at the Court-House* by setting the scene as being "a cold, wet Wednesday morning." She must not have sensed the presence of another coming upon her. For it was on this morning that young Geneva would be brutally taken from this earth.

The afternoon's *Lexington Leader* ran that day under the headline "Girl Murdered by Man in County."

On her walk to school, ten-year-old Geneva was knocked unconscious and dragged some one hundred feet away from the road. She was both assaulted and murdered in the field.

The allegation of rape never appeared in the court record, but allusions to such a heinous crime exist in several accounts. Specifically, military intelligence reports identify that the assault having been committed against the young Geneva was of a sexual nature.

Across the road from the gruesome scene, Belle McCubbing was feeding her chickens. During this daily routine, she often heard the voices of children before and after the school day. But she reported hearing nothing unusual—and certainly no sounds of distress—on the morning of February 4, 1920. Some have suggested that McCubbing not having heard any distress as being an indication that the man ultimately accused was innocent. This theory suggests that Geneva would have screamed if an unknown man suddenly appeared and then attempted to assault or harm her.

Speed Collins, a farmer in the South Elkhorn community, passed along the site where the young Geneva was first attacked as early as 7:45 a.m. Then and there, he observed a school satchel lying beside the roadside.

The South Elkhorn Schoolhouse, circa 1920. Geneva was on her way to this school when she was murdered. *University of Kentucky Libraries.*

Believing it belonged to one of the pupils at the nearby South Elkhorn School, Collins took the satchel up the hill to the schoolhouse. Geneva's teacher, Anne Young, immediately recognized the bag as belonging to Geneva Hardman.

Young considered the most likely cause of the wayward satchel: Geneva had fallen ill on the way to school. As a result, the schoolteacher dispatched a few of the older students to return the bag to Geneva at her home.

The minutes that followed are the nightmare of any parent. When her classmates arrived at the door, Mrs. Hardman answered. This much was clear: her daughter was missing. She had left for school and had neither arrived at her destination nor returned home; en route, she had lost her satchel. The *Lexington Leader* offered that "the mother immediately became alarmed and with another son and daughter started out to search."

A search was immediately begun for ten-year-old Geneva. The schoolchildren stopped at Claude Elkin's store. Elkin joined the search, along with Collins, Thomas Foley, and Geneva's mother and one of her brothers.

The search for Geneva began where Collins had found the satchel. Someone in the search party quickly noted the "tracks of a large man and

Claude B. Elkin in his store in the South Elkhorn community of Fayette County, Kentucky. *Hardman/McGregor family collection.*

The store belonging to E.B. Foley in the South Elkhorn community, circa 1900. *University of Kentucky Libraries.*

the child…on the other side of the fence in the field, where the mud was very deep, and a shallow trail indicated that her body had been dragged back into the field." The tracks, "plainly" visible, were followed. This detail of the duality of plainly visible tracks has also been identified, by some, as evidence that Geneva willingly went with whoever would be her assailant. Beyond whatever tracks may have been visible, corn fodder partially covered the body of the young girl. All was splattered in the innocent blood of a child, and a hair ribbon lay trampled in the mud. The umbrella that she had carried to protect her from the rain lay broken on the ground.

J. Winston Coleman Jr.'s *Death at the Court-House*, a booklet published in 1952 and considered to be the most complete accounting of the events described in this book, wrote that "a large, blood stained rock which had been used to crush the child's skull was found by her side. The condition of the ground has somewhat cushioned the blows of the killer, and the impression of the child's head, with one of her hair ribbons, was seen in the soft earth."

The frightful scene could have only been made worse by Mrs. Hardman being in the search party that day. The overwhelming emotion of finding one's child in such a condition is not fathomable except to those who have experienced a similar event themselves.

Reported the *Lexington Herald*: "The child's body was removed to [her] home within an hour after she had left it at 7:30 o'clock. The mother was prostrated by shock." She did not, however, grieve alone. Soon, all of central Kentucky would grieve for Geneva Hardman.

A Neighborhood Community

South Elkhorn was a tight-knit farming community in southwestern Fayette County, Kentucky. The location developed around a mill that harnessed the waters of the South Elkhorn Creek to process grain. In the vicinity, a neighborhood was established with stores, a church, and a schoolhouse. It was to this community that Emma Hardman settled her family in 1919. In the century since, the community has become a part of suburban Lexington.

Many families living in this hamlet had already been together for generations. The congregation of a Baptist church founded in 1767 in Spottsylvania County, Virginia, left its original locale in 1781. After crossing the mountains and meandering in the Kentucky wilderness for two years, most of this "travelling church" settled on the banks of the South Elkhorn Creek in Fayette County.

The restoration movement, which began at nearby Cane Ridge, Kentucky, transformed the religious landscape of central Kentucky. The Baptist "traveling church" at South Elkhorn adopted the fervor of the movement and left its Baptist roots to become in name a "Christian Church." The Hardman family participated in worship here. And it was here at the South Elkhorn Christian Church where young Geneva's funeral would be held a few days after her gruesome death just a short distance away. The church that held Geneva's funeral still stands; it was described in the Kentucky Historical Survey as a "one-and-one half story rectangular brick structure with two double-leaf doors in the gable end" resting on a stone foundation. Centrally located near the roofline of the gable end is an eight-pane rosette window. Though the exterior façade of the historic South Elkhorn sanctuary remains much the same, its interior has undergone a series of renovations following the funeral as early as 1926, and the congregation has since built additions as it has expanded and grown.

The congregation settled where some of its members constructed, also in 1783, the county's first gristmill. The location was just three miles from the

The exterior of the historic sanctuary of the South Elkhorn Christian Church (Disciples of Christ) as it appears today. The Hardman family attended this church, and Geneva's funeral was held here. *Author's collection.*

headwaters of the South Elkhorn Creek. This seemingly everlasting stream with its accessible, continuous flow was an ideal location for a gristmill.

Grist is the part of a grain that has been separated from its chaff prior to grinding. Water would be channeled through a race toward the waterwheel, which, connected to a series of gears, would ultimately turn the heavy millstone. The millstone would then grind the grist into meal or flour. The waters were so good and the soils so rich that the South Elkhorn Creek would support four gristmills by 1795. John Higbee, Colonel Abraham Bowman, Jacob Ryman and Captain James Parker each enterprised along the South Elkhorn, the first two being in the vicinity of the South Elkhorn village. Along with the gristmills came other related and accompanying businesses and stores, creating a strong micro-local economy. From 1871 until 1904, South Elkhorn even had its own post office. In the latter part of the nineteenth century, gristmills lost favor to steam power, and the need for the waters of the South Elkhorn diminished. The agrarian community, however, continued and remained close, with its two leading institutions being the church previously discussed and the schoolhouse that was Geneva's intended destination on the morning she perished.

The South Elkhorn Schoolhouse was built in the community between 1887 and 1891 as a simple one-room schoolhouse. The front door was flanked on either side by a window; admittance to the schoolhouse would have been made via a front porch. Architecturally speaking, the schoolhouse is of the Victorian vernacular style, a term that recognizes the scalloped decorative bargeboards while also acknowledging its rural simplicity. Centrally above the front door, a bell tower would have echoed throughout the community to call children to school. For nearly twenty years after Geneva's murder, pupils were taught lessons in the South Elkhorn Schoolhouse; around 1940, the rural schools throughout Fayette County were consolidated with Lexington's city schools. Although the school closed, the building still stands and is a private residence even today.

Word of the tragedy that had just befallen the Hardman family spread quickly among the neighbors. Within a short time, some fifty-plus farmers quickly assembled to search for a suspect. They carried with them shotguns and other weapons. One way or another, Geneva's death would be avenged.

Alongside the civilian posse, local authorities, including four deputies from the Fayette County sheriff's office, also descended on the scene. It is fairly certain that the deputies were not accompanied by Sheriff J. Waller Rodes. Sheriff Rodes was out of state visiting the oil fields of Texas at the time of the murder. It is unclear precisely when he returned from the Lone Star State. We do know that Rodes's signature appeared on a joint letter to

John Higbee's Mill in the vicinity of South Elkhorn as it appeared in 1921. It was one of several mills that operated along the South Elkhorn Creek. *University of Kentucky Libraries.*

Kentucky's governor signed by several local authorities on Thursday, the day following the murder. The *Lexington Herald* reported that Sheriff Rodes had been telegraphed of the heinous crime on the same day as Geneva's murder but that the telegraph was not received until the following morning. After receiving the telegraph, however, "he boarded the first train for Lexington." In any event, the sheriff recognized the need for him to return to his community as quickly as possible.

THE CHASE FOR THE ACCUSED

"News immediately spread through the settlement and a crowd of between fifty to sixty men gathered within a very few minutes," reported the *Lexington Leader* on the afternoon of the crime. At the time, Lexington had two daily newspapers. The morning *Herald* was followed each day by the afternoon *Leader*. The papers later came under common ownership and eventually merged to form the *Lexington Herald-Leader*.

Both law enforcement and the civilian posses multiplied in number as word continued to spread of the murder. Police officers and sheriff's deputies from Fayette County were joined by their colleagues from Jessamine County (and its seat, Nicholasville) and Woodford County (and its seat, Versailles). The South Elkhorn neighborhood is situated not far from the intersection of these three counties. Armed farmers joining the manhunt ultimately numbered in the hundreds.

The news reports between the competing morning *Herald* and the afternoon *Leader* may have, in some ways, inflated the response of community members, but it is clear that more people responded as news spread. We cannot know for sure how many were in the multiple search parties. However many arrived, the crowd size was suppressed because it grew only from word of mouth. The winter storms in the area over the most recent days had damaged telephone lines, so information traveled from person to person. Farmers, police officers, and sheriff deputies spread word to residents and those passing by along the roads and pikes in the vicinity.

Whoever was to catch the accused would be forced with the decision of turning him over either to the law or to lawlessness. If the civilian searchers found him, it was feared that a lynching would immediately result. A race to catch Geneva's assailant was on.

Lockett Searched for from the First

"Will Lockett was the man searched for from the first," wrote the *Lexington Herald* on Thursday morning under the headline "All-Day Pursuit Brings Capture; Negro Confesses." The column reported that all those seeking a culprit immediately focused on Will Lockett.

The first to identify Will Lockett was "Major" Woolfolk, who was traveling southbound on Harrodsburg Pike. Woolfolk—who was described by J. Winston Coleman as "an aged Negro"—told searchers that he had encountered Lockett what must have been minutes before the crime occurred, offering Lockett a ride toward Jessamine County.

Claude Elkin, who had helped find Geneva's lifeless body, reported that Lockett had visited the grocery and general store owned by he and his uncle around 7:00 a.m. Identified by both Elkin and Woolfolk, "word quickly spread that [Lockett] was the guilty man." Others at Elkin's store, too, identified Lockett as being in the vicinity that morning.

Mere presence at the scene of a crime, even when corroborated by multiple witnesses, is not conclusive of guilt. All the evidence that pointed to Lockett thus far was circumstantial. The multiple eyewitnesses identifying him in the vicinity of the crime at approximately the time of the murder could not alone establish the guilt of Will Lockett. The *Lexington Leader* stated that the "first real proof" of Lockett being the culprit, however, was at the nose of Captain Volney G. Mullikin's bloodhounds.

Captain Mullikin of the Lexington Police Department was accompanied to the South Elkhorn neighborhood by Fayette County sheriff's deputies Powell Bosworth, Cully Bryant, and Frank Hall.

Captain Mullikin and His Bloodhounds

Captain Mullikin arrived at South Elkhorn with two of his dogs. Here, he introduced his hounds to the scent of the crime scene. Captain Volney G. Mullikin was not simply a captain with the Lexington Police Department. Rather, he was an accomplished trainer of the dog breed who has been held out as "the greatest Bloodhound detective who ever lived." Over the course of his career, he counted over 2,500 convictions based at least in part on the evidence he and his dogs gathered. His most famous bloodhound, Nick Carter, accounted for nearly a quarter of those convictions, which occurred not only in Kentucky but also in other states. On one occasion, he was even hired by the Cuban government to capture a most-wanted bandit.

In *Bloodhounds and How to Train Them*, Leon Whitney recounts Mullikin's accomplishments. The shortest scent chased was about ten feet, while the longest was some fifty-five miles. On one occasion, Mullikin's hounds followed a scent for 105 hours from a burned-out henhouse to a house only a mile or so from the original crime scene after following the scent along a most circuitous route. Whitney wrote, "When the dogs stood looking at their quarry when he answered the door, and the Captain said, 'You weren't counting on the dogs when you burned that hen-house, were you?' the man said, 'No,' and thereby confessed."

With their accomplished and well-trained noses, it is not surprising, then, that Mullikin's bloodhounds immediately picked up the scent of the accused from the crime scene. The hounds' noses took them three miles to the east of South Elkhorn in the general path of Higbee Mill Road. They came upon a tobacco barn. Emerging from within were a few men who had been stripping tobacco. These men were, no doubt, alarmed at the sight of the bloodhounds and the men who followed.

Mullikin inquired of the men if they had seen any others pass by the barn and was informed, according to a report of the search in the *Lexington Leader*, that "they had seen William Lockett pass, going toward the Q and C tracks." Each of the men indicated that they "knew Lockett well" and that they had seen and recognized him from inside the barn. The news account further revealed that Lockett did not see the men. Although the men "knew Lockett well," they chose—for whatever reason—not to greet him on this rainy February morning.

The men from the tobacco barn did take note of how Lockett was dressed (in his muddied military uniform) and that "he had passed along the very route across the farm as being followed by the dogs."

Captain Mullikin's dogs "followed very closely the trail taken by him to all of these places and when the house was approached, again there was a verification of the identity of the suspect they were tracking." Such a verification would be made through the dogs' barks. The positive identification made by the men in the tobacco barn—found by the noses of Mullikin's hounds—were considered damning evidence against Will Lockett. The trail was about two hours old; Mullikin hurried his pace in the direction of the tracks.

The dogs "trailed past Republican church, where [Mullikin] took the pike and kept it for some distance then he left the pike again and took to the fields and made his way to a house not far from Republican church." At that house, a woman told Captain Mullikin that she had spoken with a black man who had passed by just thirty minutes prior. She had spoken with Lockett and then gave Captain Mullikin the man's description. It matched that given by the men from the tobacco barn of a black man wearing a dirty and tattered army uniform.

The Queen and Crescent tracks identified by the men were owned by the Southern Railway system. The tracks still exist today under the Norfolk Southern brand. The Q&C passenger line was so named because of the nicknames of the two cities it connected: the Queen City (Cincinnati) and the Crescent City (New Orleans).

The *Lexington Herald* also traced the search for Lockett. The account in the *Herald* identified a few different encounters along the trail; it also didn't identify the tracks as being those of the Q&C but rather those of the Nicholasville interurban line. The interurban lines, owned by the Kentucky Traction and Terminal Company, connected Lexington with neighboring communities of Georgetown, Paris, Nicholasville, and Frankfort. The rail lines were not the same, but they ran largely parallel to one another, with the tracks of the interurban running closer to the Nicholasville Pike. It is possible that the difference is not one at all. Rather, it could simply be an issue of sequence. Both sets of tracks could be passed while traveling westward along Brannon Road from the Nicholasville Pike. That road would cross the interurban as it made its way to the Brannon Crossing of the Q&C line.

The *Herald* reports that a farmer saw a man fitting Lockett's description walking on the Higbee Mill Pike. Next, a mailman identified as Will Hughes "declared he had seen [Lockett] on the Nicholasville Pike."

The Thursday editions of both papers report on Mullikin's interviews with those who had encountered Lockett at Brannon station. (The *Leader* identified the "people" at Brannon, while the *Herald* referred to these people as "negroes.") Those near the crossing identified Lockett as having been there for "several minutes," and they (or the newspapermen) had supposed that Lockett was waiting to board a passing train. It was about one o'clock in the afternoon. Lockett was "covered with mud to his knees," reported the *Herald*.

The various posses seemed to converge about this hour at Brannon, a northern Jessamine County village established as a railroad crossing. According to J. Winston Coleman, Fayette sheriff's deputies Powell Bosworth, Cully Bryant, and Frank Hall headed toward Brannon at this time—along with a dozen or so armed men. Two men from Versailles, Dr.

The railroad junction at Brannon of the Queen & Crescent Railroad. Will Lockett passed through here before he was captured. *University of Kentucky Libraries.*

W.T. Collette and Versailles police officer W.C. White, also here joined the search. Officer White had recently made news for capturing a truck carrying whiskey in violation of national Prohibition. (That "Great Experiment" became effective at 12:01 a.m. on Saturday, January 16, 1920.)

As the afternoon progressed, the small hamlet of Keene in western Jessamine County next drew the focus of the searchers. Dr. Collette and Officer White encountered a man walking along what is now the Keene-Troy Pike between Keene and Dixontown (the latter community being just south of Keene), inquiring of his name. The man responded that his name was "Will Hamilton." The two left him but observed him going into a residence. Collette and White moved along, believing the man was Will Hamilton.

CAPTURED IN DIXONTOWN

Wrote J. Winston Coleman, "After an all-day pursuit [of] several hundred farms and [by] officials from three counties, Lockett was captured at 4:30

28

o'clock in the afternoon at Dixontown." Collette and White grew suspicious of the identity of "Hamilton" moments after he identified himself to them. In his account of the capture of Will Lockett, William Ambrose wrote that "the pair left him on the road, but as they were driving away noted him entering a residence as if to disappear and turned around to investigate." They determined that Hamilton was in fact Lockett. When Lockett emerged from the house as their prisoner, he was still wearing his dirty army uniform. Under his arms, he carried a change of overalls to better disguise himself. The two apprehended Lockett, and minutes later, Mullikin and his hounds arrived on the scene. Captain Mullikin and his dog had tracked Lockett some seven miles in a circuitous course through southern Fayette County and northwestern Jessamine County.

The hounds following this trail would be the most damning evidence against Will Lockett. A question was asked of Lockett after his confession: "Did you account for the dogs when you murdered the little girl?"

Although the evidence was damning, the evidence might be somewhat tainted given Captain Mullikin's more complex history. In a sort of twisted justice, Mullikin was lauded as "just" with those he caught. This was the case simply because he never turned those he hunted over to a lynch mob without first eliciting a confession. This detail suggests that Mullikin might, at times, turn over the accused to a present lynch mob if such a field confession were ilicited. A twenty-first-century defense attorney would certainly use such a pattern to discredit Mullikin.

Mullikin's dual role of being 100 percent law enforcement in capacity as well as extrajudicial in some ways taints the evidence of the scent trail followed by his hounds. Would history have turned out differently had Collette and White not been the first to discover Lockett in Dixontown? Would history, at least for Lockett, have been particularly different had Mullikin simply turned him over to the yet-to-arrive-but-on-its-way mob after first extracting a confession in the field?

We cannot, however, imagine how history might have been altered by the changing of a small event or detail. The fact of the matter is that Collette and White did arrive first and they securely placed Lockett into an automobile. The accused was then driven through the South Elkhorn community en route to downtown Lexington and to the police headquarters on Water Street. News relating to his capture was not immediately released. This was done to prevent mayhem. With mobs hungry for the taste of blood searching the countryside, it would be only a matter of time before they would learn of Lockett's location. This was a reality that authorities did not wish to hasten. Lockett arrived at the station around 5:00 p.m. He was wearing his overalls over his uniform. All were caked with mud. There were spots of blood on his coat.

Will Lockett was composed during the questioning at police headquarters. His demeanor was compliant toward authorities. Other than himself, no one was there to aid Lockett during this interrogation. He had no court-appointed attorney. The Sixth Amendment to the U.S. Constitution provides for the right to counsel in "all criminal prosecutions." This, however, was a local investigation, and the Sixth Amendment applied to only federal criminal investigations until the landmark U.S. Supreme Court case *Gideon v. Wainwright* in 1963, when the Sixth Amendment was applied to felony prosecutions by the states. The Kentucky Constitution also provides for a right to counsel in all criminal prosecutions, but that right did not extend to the time of the interrogation. Until the U.S. Supreme Court's 1966 decision in *Miranda v. Arizona*, the right to remain silent was not a constitutional protection. But Will Lockett was not interrogated under our modern jurisprudence; instead, these events occurred in 1920 and it was the law of 1920 which would apply.

The first question asked of Lockett was his name. He responded that his name was "Will Lockett." When he had passed Dr. Collette and Officer White outside of Dixontown, he had given the name "Will Hamilton" and indicated that he "knew nothing of the crime."

One of the investigators inquired about a scar on Lockett's finger and whether it had been caused by self-defense on the part of young Geneva. Lockett assured them that he had received the scar "wrestling with another man." Lockett admitted to meeting Major Woolfolk, the African American man in the wagon who had first identified Lockett to investigators earlier in the morning.

"How far from there did you go before you met the girl?"

"About fifty yards."

"How did you get her over in the field?" the officers asked.

"I packed her over under my arm."

The trail originally followed by those searching for the body of Geneva Hardman had revealed two sets of foot tracks leaving the roadway; it is unclear how far the twin tracks continued off the roadway. Two feet? Twenty? If Lockett had "packed her over under" his arm, then at one point the twin tracks would have become one.

The next question asked of Lockett was whether he had "assaulted her." Clearly, a violent act had occurred against young Geneva Hardman. She had been brutally assaulted and murdered, but the question being asked was more specific and more delicate. The investigators were inquiring if Lockett had sexually assaulted ten-year-old Geneva. No doubt, her murder had incited a hunt for Geneva's assailant. Public sentiment would have been that much more violent and pressing had both her life and her "innocence" been taken.

Lockett seemed to understand the nuance of the question. Or at least that is how the exchange is portrayed by the newspapers. Lockett responded to the question of whether he had "assaulted her" by responding that he had tried to assault her but that he "didn't succeed." There was no follow-up to this line of questioning. This exchange is the only reference in the court record or in news accounts to any attempted rape or sexual assault, so it is not fully clear what Lockett meant by his response.

There is, however, one specific reference to Geneva Hardman being raped by Will Lockett. That reference is found in the general summary of the events leading up to the mob riot prepared by Major G.R.F. Cornish of the Twenty-Sixth Infantry in his intelligence report for the Military Intelligence Division (MID). There, he wrote that the trial of William Lockett was "for the murder and rape of Geneva Hardman." Again, the limited court record is not as clear in its language as was Major Cornish. Cornish did not rely on military jargon and attempted to incorporate public sentiment in his intelligence report. Was this intelligence actual, or was the inclusion of the rape charge merely the product of sentiment included in the report?

Taken together, Lockett's statements, illusory language in the newspapers, and Cornish's blunt terminology suggest that young Geneva was, in fact, the victim of a sexual assault. Knowing that the fate of Lockett would be secure with what they already had in terms of evidence, local authorities and the newspapers may have declined to press that issue. Including that specific charge or allegation might only result in even more public mayhem and a larger mob more impossible to control. Again, such a conclusion is nothing but conjecture, though it seems likely given that all of the fingers pointed in such a uniform direction.

Whatever truth may or may not surround the accusation of rape, Lockett admitted picking up "the rock used in killing her" "in the field" and that the fodder used in covering her up was obtained from the "shock where she was lying." Of the broken umbrella, investigators asked if Geneva "put up a fight, which resulted in her breaking her umbrella?" Lockett's response indicated that Geneva had stepped on the umbrella, breaking it. This response leaves room to question whether Geneva did or did not struggle. Again, no follow-up questions were asked.

Finally, Lockett was asked about motive: "What made you kill her?" To which the accused responded, "I don't know."

After the confession, Lockett was immediately transferred to the county jail that was then located on East Short Street. By 5:40 p.m., Judge-Executive Frank A. Bullock ordered that Lockett be transferred to the state reformatory in Frankfort out of concern for the accused's safety. The concern was well founded. Soon, a crowd (unaware that Lockett was no longer inside) formed outside the Fayette County jail demanding that the accused be released to the crowd. It was later reported in the *Leader* that Jailer Reuben Cropper had learned from a "reliable authority" that several in the crowd possessed dynamite. Although the atmosphere and crowd were quite literally

The old Fayette County jail on Short Street. Curiously, the county jail was located in the city, and the city jail was located in the county. *University of Kentucky Libraries.*

explosive, fortunately no spark led to violence that evening. The crowd grew in numbers so that, by 8:00 p.m., deputy jailer John P. Foster offered to allow a committee from the mob to search the jail; the offer was accepted.

The mob elected a small group of seven to conduct a detailed search of every cell in the county jail. Some reports, including J. Winston Coleman's, indicated that this "committee" was led by Ollie Troutman, a resident on Catnip Hill Road in Jessamine County who was Lockett's employer. Lockett had resided with Troutman and his wife, according to the 1920 census. But the *Lexington Herald* retracted that story days later, calling the suggestion "unfounded" yet still in reliance on a statement "given out by a county official." It would be one of several rumors that spread as events unfolded in February 1920.

Once the committee emerged from the jail without the accused, the attention of the mob shifted to the police headquarters. They incorrectly supposed that Lockett had been transferred there. Leeway was given for the mob to search that facility in the same manner.

The mob realized that Lockett was not in Lexington and made plans to go to the state capital. They "shouted: 'Let's go to Frankfort' and 'Governor Morrow will give him up to us, or we'll take him out of the pen[itentiary]'" recounted Coleman in *Death at the Court-House*. A screenplay, *Lynch Him!*, written by George Sherwood, fictionalizes all of these events. Sherwood uses a female character's voice to capture the crowd's emotion: "Any man who doesn't go to Frankfort to get that beast is a slacker."

It was estimated that some three hundred men left by private automobiles. An attempt was made to charter some of the electric interurban cars to Frankfort, but the Kentucky Traction and Terminal Company refused the transaction. About fifty men, however, did board the regularly scheduled interurban for Frankfort. Enterprising taxi drivers, however, happily took fares for the twenty-eight-mile journey to the state capital. What took place there was recorded on the pages of the *Frankfort Journal* and reprinted in the *Lexington Leader*.

As the mob arrived in Frankfort, they were met with a roadblock ordered by Governor Edwin P. Morrow. In addition to those guarding the roadway, the governor had increased the number of guards on duty at the state reformatory where Lockett was being held. "There was never any chance for the mob to have taken the Negro from the Reformatory. Governor Morrow personally mobilized the force that guarded the prison and if the mob had overrun the officers and attempted to raid the prison, its members would have been slaughtered from all sides as more than 100 men armed with

The State Penitentiary, later known as the State Reformatory, in Frankfort, circa 1911. *Capital City Museum, Frankfort, Kentucky.*

shotguns were standing at their posts to protect the prison and ready to fire at the command of Governor Morrow."

One vehicle, taking a different route, did make it to Frankfort. In fact, it made it all the way to the reformatory. The occupants of the vehicle—James Bradley of South Elkhorn, Walker Nelson of Lexington, and Newt Schooler of Versailles—were promptly arrested and "taken into the presence of Governor Morrow." The following account is from the *Frankfort Journal*:

> *"What do you then want here?" asked Governor Morrow.*
>
> *"We came to see if you would not give us that nigger," they replied.*
>
> *"Are you armed?" asked Governor Morrow.*
>
> *The men replied that they were not armed, but that they were searched and when it was found that they were not armed, Governor Morrow bade them sit down. He told them that he would not permit them to be released until later that night. One of the men, Mr. Bradley, said he was a relative of the child who had been murdered.*
>
> *"Tell the mother of this poor child," said Governor Morrow, "that the*

law will be enforced in this case. There will be no miscarriage of justice for her. Tell this poor woman that the man who killed her little child will be punished to the full extent of the law.

The men were satisfied by Governor Morrow's assurances. Morrow took an incredibly involved role in the events of the evening. After meeting with the men, the governor traveled by automobile to the hill, where he intended on disbursing the mob. There, he learned that the mob had already been sent home by the sheriff of Franklin County largely without incident.

Part Three

THAT LAW AND ORDER MIGHT PREVAIL

GOVERNOR EDWIN P. MORROW

When Governor Morrow met with the men at the reformatory, he had not been the chief executive of the Commonwealth of Kentucky for long. Edwin Porch Morrow was elected governor of the commonwealth in the election of 1919 by defeating the sitting governor, James D. Black. Black, a Democrat who ascended to the governorship when Augustus O. Stanley resigned to take a seat in the U.S. Senate, lost the 1919 election by some 40,000 votes on charges of corruption. Morrow, a progressive Republican, had previously run for governor in 1915 against Stanley but narrowly lost that election by 417 votes.

Morrow was born in Somerset on November 28, 1877, to one of the founding families of the Republican Party in Kentucky. His father, Thomas Zanzinger Morrow, was among the twenty-eight men who formed the political party. He was a staunch supporter of Abraham Lincoln's 1860 presidential campaign and would ultimately serve in both houses of the Kentucky legislature as well as in the judiciary as a circuit court judge. In 1883, Thomas Z. Morrow was the Republican nominee for governor. Although Edwin Morrow's father never found himself in the governor's mansion, Edwin's uncle did: William O'Connell Bradley (the brother of Virginia Catherine Bradley, Morrow's mother) was elected in 1895 and was the first Republican governor of Kentucky.

Edwin P. Morrow was elected in 1919 as Kentucky's fortieth governor. He is shown here in 1918 addressing soldiers who would be sent to fight in the First World War. *University of Kentucky Libraries*.

Morrow left Somerset to attend St. Mary's College in Lebanon, Kentucky, and later Cumberland College, which is located in Williamsburg, Kentucky. Finally, he matriculated to the University of Cincinnati, where he obtained a law degree in 1902. Thereafter, Edwin Morrow settled in Lexington, where the future governor opened his law office in the McClelland Building at 163 West Short Street. A few months into the practice of law, Judge Watts Parker tapped Morrow to represent William Moseby in the accused's second trial of the murder of a prominent citizen in the community. The case would immeasurably raise the young attorney's stature in the community and among fellow members of the bar.

That murder had occurred in December 1900, when Jesse N. Hawkins was robbed and killed on Second Street. Hawkins had served as the treasurer of his church, and it was reported that he had several thousand dollars of church funds on his person when he was murdered. The sensational murder received much attention in the press both locally and beyond. The accused confessed; despite this confession, a hung jury resulted from the initial trial. The commonwealth sought to retry the case, though no attorney would take the mantle of representing William Moseby. Judge Parker, desperate to offer the accused an attorney, turned to a young lawyer whom he believed could not say no. The judge was correct, but he—as well as the whole community—could not have anticipated the extraordinary defense offered. Morrow "soon showed that Moseby's confession had been extorted, and that a very great deal of the testimony as presented was faulty," wrote Willard Jillson in his biographical sketch of the governor.

Jillson went on to write that Morrow's star was rising. There was a "greater and much more important group of men before whose eyes [Morrow's] reputation had risen suddenly like a new, bright star on a midsummer night to join that brilliant, well known constellation of grandfather, father, and uncle." The ambition of this star, however, remained committed to the plight of those who, like Moseby, might otherwise have no voice and no representation.

Edwin Morrow returned to his hometown of Somerset and was hired as the city attorney. In 1910, President William Howard Taft appointed Morrow the U.S. District Attorney for the Eastern District of Kentucky. For this assignment, Morrow relocated to the city of Covington, Kentucky. He served until the political winds shifted. As a Republican appointee, Morrow's services were no longer needed during the administration of President Woodrow Wilson. Morrow returned to private practice, in Somerset, and continued to seek his own political advancement.

For the 1919 gubernatorial election, Jillson wrote, Morrow campaigned on the platform that he "was not bound to any man, or group of men. He had made no pledges nor promises to secure his nomination, and none had been made for him." This, in and of itself, was a campaign promise against the corruption being alleged against Governor Black, a Democrat. In launching his campaign at Pikeville on September 8, 1919, Morrow promised "to bring a new and better day to Kentucky." His inaugural address sought God's guidance for the "strength to do the right" and for sustenance "in the administration of law and justice."

The administration of law and justice would prove to be one of Governor Edwin Morrow's most shining legacies. The *New York Evening World* commented that Morrow "seems to be a man with a brain and a spinal column, both in good working order and in their proper places." Morrow exercised both of these faculties during the events that unfolded in Lexington in early 1920; his role cannot be overstated.

Grand Jury Indicts

On the morning of February 5, 1920, the Fayette County grand jury issued an indictment against Will Lockett for the murder of Geneva Hardman the day before. The grand jury's indictment found that Lockett "with force and arms, did unlawfully, willfully, maliciously, feloniously and of his malice aforethought, kill, slay and murder Geneva Hardman by striking, wounding and beating the said Geneva Hardman with a stone, a deadly weapon, from which striking, wounding and beating the said Geneva Hardman then and there died."

The indictment was brought by John R. Allen, the commonwealth's attorney. Testifying witnesses before the grand jury included Dr. Collette, Officer White, Ernest Thompson, Dudley Veal, Lexington police chief Jere Reagan, Joseph Woolfolk, Claude Elkin, and D.C. Elkin. A public statement by Chief Reagan included in Coleman's *Death at the Court-House* described the crime "as the most brutal ever perpetrated in Fayette County."

The issuance of a true bill of an indictment was a preliminary step to determine if there was sufficient evidence to bring formal charges against Lockett. The work of a grand jury is conducted in secret. If a grand jury does not return an indictment after finding a sufficiency of evidence to bring charges, then the individual accused should not have his or her name impugned by publicity of those proceedings. Although there may have been secrecy surrounding the proceedings against Will Lockett, they were quickly exposed to light when the true bill was issued. The jury determined that there was sufficient evidence to proceed to trial.

Even with the justice system progressing at a hurried pace, the mob action of the previous evening did not abate. Judge Charles Kerr recognized that in order that justice might prevail through the avoidance of an unjust lynching of the accused, he scheduled the trial for Monday, February 9, during the court's regular session. Some have confused the regular session of the circuit court with "court day." At the time, the former occurred twice monthly and was the date when judicial proceedings occurred. The latter, however, was then a monthly event that occurred next to the courthouse on Cheapside. It was an occasion when those from throughout the county could come to a central location to socialize and to shop and trade. (Today, we might even think of this as a farmers' market, similar to what happens every Saturday at Lexington's Cheapside. Cheapside also has a quite nefarious past, as it was the location of Lexington's slave trade as well.)

FAYETTE CIRCUIT COURT

THE COMMONWEALTH OF KENTUCKY }

against

Will Lockett.   } Murder.

The Grand Jury of Fayette County, in the name and by the authority of the Commonwealth of Kentucky, accuse Will Lockett

of the crime of murder

committed as follows, viz: that said Will Lockett

on the 4th **day of** February   19?0 **in the county aforesaid** and before the finding of this indictment, with force and arms, did unlawfully, willfully, maliciously, feloniously and of his malice aforethought, kill, slay and murder Geneva Hardman by striking, wounding and beating the said Geneva Hardman with a stone, a deadly weapon, from which striking, wounding and beating the said Geneva Hardman then and there died,

against the peace and dignity of the Commonwealth of Kentucky.
             JOHN R. ALLEN, Commonwealth's Attorney.

Witness: Malcolm Brown. *Dr WT Collette, W C. White, E Thompson, Dud Veal, Jas Woolfolk J J Rogan C E Elkin D C Elkin*   *Feb. 2-5-20*

The indictment brought by the grand jury against Will Lockett for the murder of Geneva Hardman. *Kentucky Department for Library and Archives.*

Also on Thursday, February 5, local officials sent a letter to Governor Morrow requesting state assistance in keeping the peace for the Monday trial.

We…would respectfully request to your Excellency, that in our judgment it will be necessary and expedient for you to direct the State Militia, or such State Constabulary or National Guard as you may have at your command, sufficient in number to render ample protection to the Court and prisoner, to accompany one Will Lockett from the City of Frankfort, to this City… and be present during his trial in this Court, charged with the offense of Murder. This representation and request is made for the reason that the crime of which he is charged is one that has created great public excitement

Cheapside as it appeared in 1921, as seen looking west from the courthouse. The photographer, Asa C. Chinn, photographed Lexington's downtown streetscapes for insurance purposes. *University of Kentucky Libraries.*

Circuit Judge,

Commonwealths Attorney.

County Judge.

Sheriff.

The signatures of Fayette County's circuit judge, commonwealth's attorney, county judge, and sheriff on a letter to Governor Morrow requesting the presence of troops in Lexington, Kentucky, on the day of the Lockett trial. *Kentucky Department for Library and Archives.*

and indignation, in so much so that thousands of citizens gathered at the jail in this City, intent on taking him from the officials having him in charge and publicly executing him. That feeling has been allayed, but feeling is so intense we fear there may be a reprisal of the feeling exhibited at the time of his arrest, necessitating his removal to the State Reformatory. The trial has been set for February 9th, at 9 o'clock A.M.

This letter was signed by four locally elected officials: Circuit Court Judge Charles Kerr, Commonwealth's Attorney John Allen, County Judge-Executive Fred Bullock, and Sheriff J.W. Rodes. Local officials knew that the community was a powder keg, and they sought the necessary assistance from the state to keep it from exploding.

A CALL FOR PEACE

Thursday afternoon, the *Lexington Leader* editorialized the sentiment for civility under the caption "Let Law and Order Prevail." The editorial comment observed that "the good name of the community" had prevailed through Lockett's arrest and through the initial protection of the accused. It then demanded that the "self-confessed murderer be given the due process of public trial" and predicted that "justice will be swift and certain." It seemed that the prevailing belief was of both certainty of a guilty verdict and that there would be trouble at the courthouse. The *Leader*'s Sunday headline summarized all the effort in place to keep the peace:

Troops with Machine Guns and Automatic Rifles, Special Deputy Sheriffs, City and County Officers to Protect Lockett

The *Lexington Herald* proclaimed in a front-page headline on Friday, February 6, 1920: "Swift Action Is Promised for Trial of Confessed Slayer of Young Girl." A brief trial was to occur "in the same county in which the crime was committed and within five days from its perpetration," and the accused "Will Lockett, negro, confessed murderer of 10-year-old Geneva Hardman, will be tried Monday morning at 9 o'clock in the Fayette Circuit Court." In addition to being a "brief trial," as noted by the newspaper, it was also expedient in terms of time elapsed since the commission of the crime. Today, we look back at this timeline in shock. But such a swift trial calendar in 1920, although unusual, would not be considered extreme. And local authorities believed that a quick trial served the common good by keeping the peace.

"Trial within a few days' time of the crime and in the same county should have the effect of discouraging mob violence by allowing justice to take an unusually swift course," said Judge Charles Kerr the afternoon after the murder took place. It had been contemplated that the venue should be changed for the trial, but the decision to keep the proceedings in Fayette County was made by Judge Kerr and Judge-Executive Fred Bullock.

On the front page of the *Herald*'s Sunday edition, a statement by Tupper Hardman was printed under the headline "Brother of Dead Child Decries Mob Violence." The *Leader* also carried Tupper Hardman's statement that was made on behalf of his entire family. Tupper was a successful farmer in Fayette County with property throughout the county; as previously noted, he had at various times owned property off both the Tates Creek and Harrodsburg Pikes. Although he would lose many of his landholdings at the end of the decade, he was very well respected in the community and the patriarch of the family at the time of Geneva's murder. His statement read:

> *As a brother of Geneva Hardman, who was murdered by Will Lockett, and as a representative of her family, I request all of our friends and those who sympathize with us not to indulge in any violence or create any disturbance when Lockett is brought here for trial. The authorities have acted promptly, the man is under arrest, he has been indicted promptly and his trial fixed for next Monday.*
>
> *There is no doubt of his guilt and he has confessed to it, and I feel sure that a prompt and speedy trial will take place and that any jury empaneled will find him guilty and punish him adequately for the horrible crime he has committed.*
>
> *The precipitation of a battle or conflict between the authorities protecting the man and citizens who are justly indignant over the crime would necessarily result in many deaths and probably the killing of innocent bystanders who are taking no part in the conflict.*
>
> *I would hate to see the life of any other person endangered or lost as the result of violence by reason of a conflict over a brute like this and I, therefore, urge all citizens, for the good name of the county and in the interest of law and order, to do nothing to interfere with the orderly processes of the law, because I am confident that prompt and exact justice will be done, and that punishment commensurate with the crime will be meted out to this man.*

These words were later recognized by many for their eloquence and sense of calm given the awful tragedy that had just befallen his family. They also proved an ominous hint of what would come the next morning.

Local authorities had prepared for the possibility of violence, and state guardsmen were present as well following the request for aid made by local officials to Governor Morrow. The headline of the *Lexington Herald* conveyed confidence: "Authorities Are Confident Trial of Slayer Monday Will Be Orderly." Over fifty special police officers were sworn in, and Morrow answered the call of local officials by sending the home guard to protect the prisoner and keep the peace. The desire of both state and local officials had been to bring in regular troops for the trial, but doing so would have required Governor Morrow to declare that a state of lawlessness already existed. Despite the fomenting anger, the rule of law still reigned for the moment in Lexington and throughout Fayette County. Instead, Adjutant General James M. Deweese, commander of the home guard, assembled the men of Company D under the direct command of Captain L.V. Crockett to man the battle stations around the old courthouse. General Deweese also issued a statement that was printed in the newspaper for the people of Lexington to see:

> *Warning is hereby given to all persons that any attempt by individuals or groups to obstruct the civil authorities in the performance of their duty or to penetrate the zone fixed by the military authorities will be met with force.*
>
> *Additional warning is given herewith that loitering or lingering about the approaches to the courthouse will place those persons in the danger zone should a resort to force be necessary. Individuals or groups will do this at their own peril.*
>
> *The responsibility for any bloodshed at this trial will rest on those who disregard their duty as citizens and attempt to take the law out of the hands of the constituted authorities.*
>
> *It is confidently expected that the citizens of Fayette County will respect the law as administered by their own officials and entities.*
>
> *James M. Deweese, the Adjutant General*

Other organizations also called for peace. Two African American groups, the Civic League and the Ministers' Alliance, both sought swift justice against the accused. Sunday sermons in Lexington included calls for restraint among congregants. Among those making such requests from the pulpit was Dr. Elmer E. Snoddy. Dr. Snoddy served as the senior minister at both Shannondale Christian Church and South Elkhorn Christian Church. The former is a small church near the community now known as "Little Texas," about three miles out Military Pike from South Elkhorn. And it was at South Elkhorn Christian Church, of course, that Snoddy ministered to the bereaved Hardman family and officiated at Geneva's funeral. At Shannondale, Dr. Snoddy spoke on the "observance of the law."

A Sunday editorial, under the caption "Let the Law Take Its Course," in the *Lexington Leader* sought nothing more than the law to be upheld. In specific terms, the protection of the accused was directly sought: "Any man other than an officer acting under instructions of the courts who should do violence to William Lockett, who would unlawfully deprive him of his life, in the eyes of the laws of God and man, be guilty of murder." To protect Lockett, according to the *Leader*, was of the upmost importance.

Protecting Will Lockett, however, should not be elevated to some grand effort to either save a man's life or even to truly protect the rule of law. With Lockett's conviction a foregone conclusion, the effort to save and protect Will Lockett was intended more so to uphold the appearance of the rule of law.

The *Lexington Leader* reported in its Sunday edition that Lockett would be accompanied on a special train that would arrive in Lexington from the state reformatory in Frankfort at 9:00 a.m. This report was a ruse; it was fake news. Lockett had arrived in town about five hours earlier via an automobile caravan. In the vehicle with Lockett were Adjutant General Deweese as well as Major Isaac Wilder. Sheriff Rodes and three of his deputies also joined the caravan, which was protected by a convoy of three army trucks carrying Company D troops. The third-floor circuit courtroom in the old courthouse had a prisoner's cell to which Lockett was immediately taken on his arrival at the Fayette County Courthouse.

While the people of Lexington slept, the police began stretching steel cables around the courthouse to prevent any crowd from pressing into the public square; keeping angry mobs at a distance from the courthouse was the priority. The entrances to the building, save one, were locked, and machine guns commanded all entrances. Troops patrolled the streets.

When the people of Lexington awoke on the morning of February 9, 1920, the area around the public square looked, and no doubt felt, radically different than it had at any point in Lexington's history. Only those who could recall troops present during the Civil War some fifty-five years earlier might have memories of such a show of force here. Morning had broken in Lexington, Kentucky. It would be a day unlike any other.

THE OLD COURTHOUSE

An automobile departed Frankfort at about 1:15 in the early-morning hours. Inside the vehicle was the accused, Will Lockett, who was accompanied by Sheriff Rodes. The vehicle traveled along the old Frankfort Pike without issue and was accompanied by ninety-seven soldiers of Company D of the Kentucky National Guard based out of Covington. They and others would guard the courthouse during the day.

Soldiers were also set to guard the courthouse during the Monday morning trial. These soldiers, some three hundred strong, were state guardsmen, also known as the home guard. They were tasked with protecting the three-story Richardsonian-Romanesque courthouse, which had been open for only twenty years at the time of the trial. The courthouse it replaced was short-lived; it had burned in an accidental fire. This "new" courthouse, today known in Lexington as the "old" courthouse, was designed by the Cleveland, Ohio–based architecture firm Lehman & Schmitt. The building was constructed for $187,000; $68,000 was spent on furnishings. Noted architect and architectural historian Clay Lancaster described the grand building in his book *Vestiges of the Venerable City*:

> *In its rough and smooth gray stonework, stress on horizontals, arched windows, and prominent dormers, the new courthouse reflects the former post office* [located at Main and what is now Martin Luther King Boulevard]. *But its form is symmetrical and the ground story is given a basement treatment, with the monumental front staircase ascending to the round-arched doorway. The clerestory with corner turret-buttresses is reminiscent of the superstructure of Richardson's Trinity Church in Boston, which was modeled after the twelfth-century tower of the cathedral at Salamanca in Spain. A clock is set in a dormer on each side, and the eight-sided dome rises to a small circular colonnetted pavilion at the top.*

This magnificent courthouse where Will Lockett was tried still stands. It was (in the words of Lancaster) "mutilated" by a 1966 renovation, though that renovation also saved the old courthouse from demolition and could be considered a successful "adaptive reuse" of sorts. It left the framework for a revitalization in 2018 that has transformed the structure into a modernized version of its former glory. The beautiful restoration allows for the details on the old courthouse to be more visible, as a century's worth of grime has been removed. Giant urns on either side of the exterior staircase facing

Completed in 1898, the fourth courthouse for Fayette County served the county until new courthouses opened along North Limestone Street in 2002. *University of Kentucky Libraries.*

Main Street proclaim "law" and "justice" to those entering the front doors. To those departing, the message is of "liberty" and "peace." The sculptor of these details and others around the building was Frederick Bullen Miles, an English native who moved to Asheville, North Carolina. He was one of many artisans who labored on the Biltmore mansion, and his work can be found on landmarks across the southern United States.

Outside this imposing structure, the guardsmen and police assembled around the courthouse. It was a substantial crowd. Although administrators had discouraged students from attending, many collegians from both the University of Kentucky and Transylvania College could not keep away from the excitement.

Adjutant General James M. Deweese surveys the preparations for the Lockett trial from behind the wire cable. *J. Winston Coleman Photo Collection, Transylvania University Library.*

The mob outside the Fayette County Courthouse during the trial of Will Lockett. *J. Winston Coleman Photo Collection, Transylvania University Library.*

State guardsmen, with bayonets fixed, keep the lynch mob from advancing on the courthouse. *J. Winston Coleman Photo Collection, Transylvania University Library.*

Members of the mob mill about on Main Street prior to the Second Battle of Lexington. *J. Winston Coleman Photo Collection, Transylvania University Library.*

Heavy steel wires, or cables, had been constructed along the sidewalks around the courthouse at waist height to keep the crowd back. This work was done under the cloak of darkness at "about 1 o'clock this morning by a crew from police headquarters," according to the morning's *Herald*. The *Herald* also reported the following efforts taken to secure the courthouse and protect the proceedings:

> *Soldiers and members of the police department will guard these lines to see that only persons whose business requires their entrance to the blocked zone are permitted inside the wires.*
>
> *Notice was given to the central fire department station late last night that Upper street and Cheapside from Main to Short streets would be closed to traffic and a detour would be necessary in case of an alarm.*
>
> *The cables will be removed and the streets opened to traffic just as soon after the trial as conditions will permit.*

There was one young couple having business requiring entrance to that secure zone and into the courthouse. E.R. Grace and Minnie Cunningham traveled that morning from Covington, Kentucky, unaware of the excitement occurring in Lexington. They were eloping and arrived at the courthouse to obtain their marriage license. Together, they crossed the line and were admitted to the courthouse on what would no doubt be a most memorable wedding day. They were married by Reverend Clarence Walker of the Ashland Avenue Baptist Church and "lost no time in leaving the city" after the ceremony was over.

THE JURORS

On either side of the Short Street entrance to the old courthouse are the faces of six men, twelve in total, who are said to represent the twelve men of the jury. When Miles sculpted the faces of the jury members, women were not permitted to serve on juries. By the time of Lockett's trial, it was possible that a woman could be seated on the jury. In January 1920, Kentucky ratified the Nineteenth Amendment to the Constitution, giving women the right to vote; with that right came a woman's right to serve on juries. Although possible, it was unlikely that a woman would be appointed to serve on a jury for a capital offense, especially one as gruesome as this. And in reality, both public (and judicial) sentiment and patriarchy still reigned supreme. The *New York Times*, in 1927, published an article claiming that "fainting fits and outbursts of tears" would result if women were empaneled on juries. As a result, it was customary for juries to be composed almost exclusively of prominent, white men. The trial of Will Lockett was no different.

The process of selecting the twelve jurors for the matter of *Commonwealth v. William Lockett* took only twelve minutes. And this was nearly half of the entire time dedicated to the entire trial. The process of jury selection is known as *voir dire*; it gives both judges and attorneys the opportunity to question potential jurors for prejudices, biases, and conflicts. The selection of the jury was the first order of business on Monday morning.

On behalf of Will Lockett, George R. Hunt rose. He asked the jury a single question. His words indicated the plea which was to come and suggested that there would be little defense on behalf of the accused. "Admitting the guilt of the defendant, do you think you can try this case fairly and impartially?" All agreed they could. It was clear with Hunt's words that Lockett would admit his guilt and that sentencing would be the main question to be answered by the twelve men on the jury.

It was the case, however, that one juror was not selected because of the response he gave to a question posited during *voir dire* by the commonwealth's attorney, John R. Allen. John Lewis Christopher had "conscientious scruples against capital punishment" and thus was dismissed from service on the jury. Christopher, a native of Garrard County, Kentucky, had moved to Lexington in 1901. In matters of politics, he was a Republican; in matters of faith, he was a Methodist. Soon after his arrival, he served as a Republican precinct captain in the South Elkhorn neighborhood, where he would reside through the 1920 census. In other words, Christopher lived not particularly far from the scene of the crime. Witnesses to the crime and perhaps members of the victim's family could have been familiar to him. For him to take such a stand was a noble position, especially for the time and under the circumstances. As the *Herald* put it, "only one man" had such reservations. It was a reference to the jury pool and those answering the questions of attorney Allen. It seemed as if, in that moment, only John Lewis Christopher carried such a conviction against capital punishment as it pertained to Will Lockett.

Because of his convictions, John Lewis Christopher was dismissed from service and was not seated on the jury. Instead, the following twelve men were selected: John G. Stoll (foreman), David A. Crosby, John G.

Cramer, William C. McDowell, W.S. Burrier, Thomas Rhorer, T.E. Henton, James H. Curry, Henry C. Downing, George T. Hukle, Frank Battaile, and R.L. Henderson.

The jury foreman was the owner of the daily *Lexington Leader*, a former member of the Kentucky House of Representatives, president of the Lexington Water Company, and had served in the leadership of several other local business entities. John Stoll was a well-regarded philanthropist, an active progressive-minded Republican, and a respected member in the community. In time, he would acquire the *Herald*, bringing the two main daily newspapers under common ownership, which set the stage for the newspapers to eventually merge.

D.A. Crosby has been misidentified by virtually every account to wit as "J.A. Crosby." The court records properly identify the initial as a *D*, which would belong to David A. Crosby, president of the Union Transfer & Storage Company. Crosby resided on the pike to Bowman's Mil in the South Elkhorn community on a farm that he and his mother had acquired in 1909. Crosby, a native of Shelby County, graduated in 1897 from the Sims Medical School in St. Louis, but he ceased practicing medicine on his relocation to the old Woolfolk Farm. He never married. Long after the trial, Judge Charles Kerr described Crosby as having a "fine country home" where he introduced a "system and efficiency into the farming operations."

William. S. Burrier, like David Crosby, resided in the South Elkhorn neighborhood.

John G. Cramer lived on Elsmere Park with his wife; at the time he was the secretary and treasurer of the Phoenix Hotel (the successor to Postlethwaite's Tavern and the oldest hostelry in the city). Another noted civic leader, Cramer had chaired a Masonic committee in 1908 to secure funds for the repair of the statue of Henry Clay that tops the late leader's mausoleum at the Lexington Cemetery. In 1939, Cramer enlisted public support for repairs to the landmark.

William Cochran McDowell, thirty-one, and his wife rented a home on Headley Avenue on Lexington's north side. Together, they had a six-year-old daughter, Alice. His father was a railroad titan, his grandfather was Major McDowell and his grandmother was a granddaughter of Henry Clay. At the time of the trial, McDowell was a manager on a tobacco farm; he would later go into real estate and develop much of the land that had been part of Henry Clay's Ashland estate.

Thomas Rhorer's identity must be that of John Thomas Rhorer, the only Thomas Rhorer in Fayette County as of the 1920 census. (The timing of the trial and the census coincided in such a way as to greatly aid the identification of each of these jurors.) Rhorer was a farmer who resided in northern Fayette County on Lemon's Mill Pike.

"T.E. Hinton" is identified in the official court report as a juror, and Winston Coleman gives us a first name: Thomas. But census records do not show a Thomas Hinton in Lexington; they do, however, identify a Thomas Henton. Thomas E. Henton, to be precise. It is this author's belief that although Coleman likely knew Henton, he carried forward the scrivener's error from the official court documents in his book. Henton, forty-seven, was an operator with the Gentry-Thompson Stockyards Company and would rise to become its president in 1938. His obituary read that he was a "pioneer in the livestock auctions industry" who established the "present system of selling in Lexington in 1921."

James H. Curry, thirty-one, lived on Woodland Avenue in Lexington and was the proprietor of a soft drink stand licensed to operate at 109 North Mill Street. By all accounts, Curry was an honest and law-abiding man. While several other soft drink stand operators in town wrestled with charges of bootlegging and other Prohibition-related crimes, Curry's record remained clean.

Henry C. Downing farmed on property he owned along the Tates Creek Road. The thirty-nine-year-old was from a prominent Lexington family that had its own series of tragedies. By the time of the trial, two of Downing's children had died at an early age. In 1948, he committed suicide near the toolshed on his farm by shooting himself in the neck with a shotgun. Seven years later, his widow committed suicide by jumping from the Clay's Ferry Bridge.

George T. Hukle was a fifty-eight-year-old mechanic who had once lived in the South Elkhorn neighborhood decades before the arrival of the Hardman family in the neighborhood.

Frank Battaile was the manager of a bookstore in 1920, living with his in-laws on West Second Street in the home where former Vice President John C. Breckinridge had resided following the Civil War. He would die in an automobile accident in 1926.

Robert Letcher Henderson was the thirteenth juror, his seat on the empaneled jury being available only by John Lewis Christopher's opposition to the use of capital punishment. His family had arrived in Fayette County in 1790, settling the Muir Station area of the county. A farmer, he still worked the old family land until his death in 1933.

Of the lot, they were uniformly male and uniformly Caucasian. At least two hailed from the South Elkhorn precinct. Others had previously lived in the vicinity of the victim's home. The relative uniformity among the jurors is a natural result of our jury system, as they were simply residents of the community. An overly homogenous population will naturally result in a relatively homogenous juror pool. And a pool selected in a relatively small town—like Lexington in 1920—is unlikely to entirely comprise wholly unconnected individuals. Jury composition, particularly in rural areas, remains an issue in Kentucky.

JUDGE CHARLES KERR

Charles Kerr presided over the Lockett trial. He was a circuit court judge who had served in that capacity since his appointment in 1911 by Governor Augustus E. Wilson following the death of Kerr's predecessor, Judge Watts Parker. In politics, Kerr was a Republican, though he had been a Democrat until 1896. He was born in the Ohio River city of Maysville, Kentucky. In the middle of the Civil War, he and his family relocated to Fayette County. The young Kerr worked on the family farm until he began studying law under the tutelage of W.C.P. Breckinridge and John T. Shelby. In 1886, Kerr began his law practice after passing the Kentucky bar exam. Kerr was best known for his oratorical skills and was "practically" the unanimous choice of the Fayette County Bar Association for the 1911 appointment to the position by Governor Wilson. Charles Kerr was "a sound and safe lawyer, clear in thought and logical in his mental processes…and patient and careful in his study and investigation of question submitted for his counsel."

In addition to his oratorical skills and logical mind, Kerr was a passionate historian. He served as the editor of a five-volume history of Kentucky, one of the first significant works on the commonwealth's origins and early settlements. His role as editor for two professional historians evidenced his stature in that field as well. The Sunday following Geneva's murder, being the day before the trial, a lengthy column written by Judge Kerr was printed in the *Lexington Herald* titled "The Fatalism of Lincoln."

Fatalism is the philosophical belief that all events are predetermined and, therefore, cannot be avoided. Kerr's writing was about the late president's belief in fatalism and that he, Lincoln, was not "the product of mere chance." Kerr recounted Lincoln's childhood copybook in which young Abraham wrote, "Abraham Lincoln/his hand and pen,/he will be good/but God knows when." Lincoln believed that "the past is the cause of the present, and the present will be the cause of the future." The rise of Lincoln—from a poor boyhood to the executive mansion and from a lanky electoral failure to "one of the greatest of the worlds immortals"—was simply the result of cause and effect. Lincoln's philosophical outlook suggested that it was not any action taken by or caused by himself that resulted in the outcomes of his own life or in the cause of preservation of the union, but simply a cause and an effect predestined to occur. Judge Kerr reflected on these things but never fully tipped his own hand as to whether he joined Abraham Lincoln in adhering to this belief system.

Did Judge Kerr also believe in fatalism? His writings in the *Herald* on the eve of the trial certainly allude to a fatalistic result for Will Lockett and the upcoming trial. From the moment the investigation into who killed Geneva Hardman turned toward Lockett, his death by all accounts was almost a foregone conclusion. The only question of Lockett's fate was in reality the method and legality of his execution. Although the lynch mob had sought to execute its own justice, local authorities, including Kerr, sought to postpone Lockett's fate to allow the legal process to run its course.

J. Winston Coleman, without using the term *fatalism*, summarized the scene in this way: "everyone agreed that there could be but one outcome of the trial—speedy conviction and a death sentence. But the main issue to be decided was whether the sentence would be carried out legally, or by a mob."

Judge Kerr arrived at the courthouse around 8:00 a.m. the morning of the trial. Judge-Executive Bullock had already been in the building for about an hour.

ALL RISE

Typically, multiple entrances to the courthouse would have been open for those seeking to conduct their business there. The county courthouse did not simply serve a judicial function; it also housed local government offices, where deeds and marriage licenses were recorded and property taxes assessed, as well as the fiscal court, which caused the county to function.

But this ordinarily accessible building was tightly secured on the morning of February 9, 1920. Only the Main Street entrance was open; it stood at the top of a flight of stone steps.

At 9:00 a.m. Monday morning, Judge Kerr took the bench in the courtroom and opened the trial in the matter of *The Commonwealth of Kentucky vs. Will Lockett* on the sole count of murder. Deputy Sheriff Malcolm Brown called for silence so that the names of the twelve prospective jurors could be heard as he called them out to take their places in the jury box. The courtroom was filled and had been so for the fifteen minutes preceding the trial, but it was not overflowing. Careful attention was made by Sheriff Rodes and other authorities to admit into the courtroom only enough persons to fill the seats. "None were permitted to stand in the aisles or along the walls," wrote J. Winston Coleman. As silence was demanded in the courtroom, the sounds from the mob outside grew louder.

The first fifteen minutes were committed to the selection of the jury through the *voir dire* process before the prosecution and defense would offer their respective cases. In Kentucky, there are two types of prosecutors in criminal cases. A county attorney generally serves as the prosecutor in misdemeanor cases in district court. Meanwhile, the commonwealth's attorney prosecutes felonies in circuit court. In either type of case, the state, or in this case the commonwealth, has the burden of proof and must prove the guilt of a defendant "beyond a reasonable doubt." To meet this high burden, the facts as presented must be so damning that there can be no plausible explanation other than the guilt of the defendant. It would therefore be the burden of the commonwealth to prove the guilt of Will Lockett. Lockett's preliminary admission through his lawyer during jury selection, however, shifted the burden; through his admission, the case was already won for the commonwealth.

Seated at the table for the prosecution were Commonwealth's Attorney John R. Allen and County Attorney Hogan Yancey; they were also joined by Buckner Allen, who was another member of the Fayette bar and the brother of the commonwealth's attorney. As this was a felony case, Allen served as lead prosecutor. When asked by the court, the prosecution indicated that it was ready to proceed against the defendant.

Judge Kerr then looked toward Lockett's defense counsel to determine their readiness for the proceedings.

A RIGHT TO COUNSEL

The two men seated at the table for the defense were Colonel Samuel M. Wilson and George R. Hunt. Coleman identified the two attorneys as "two of the ablest members of the Fayette bar." Judge Kerr appointed these two attorneys to represent the accused.

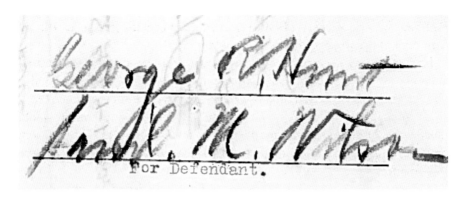

The signatures of Lockett's two attorneys, George R. Hunt and Samuel M. Wilson, as they appeared on the demurrer to the indictment filed on behalf of their client. *Kentucky Department for Library and Archives*.

Wilson had served as a judge-advocate in the First World War. His most famous case was his defense of Caleb Powers. Powers, the Kentucky secretary of state, was on multiple occasions tried and convicted (and his convictions overturned on appeal) for complicity in the assassination of Governor William Goebel. In his autobiographical account of the trials against him, Powers described Wilson as having made the "ablest argument" in his defense. Ultimately, Powers would receive a pardon before being elected to multiple terms in Congress. Samuel Wilson maintained a successful law practice in Lexington and also was a scholar of Lexington and early Kentucky history; later in his career, he would be appointed by the U.S. Supreme Court to serve as a special master in a border dispute between the states of Kansas and Missouri.

Lockett's other attorney, George R. Hunt, had previously served as Fayette County's attorney through political appointment. Hunt was very active in Democratic politics and became chair of the local party the year following the Lockett trial. At one point, however, he was challenged by party loyalists for his willingness to vote cross-ticket for what he perceived to be a better candidate.

These two distinguished barristers were appointed to represent Lockett, although there is some question as to when their appointment occurred. Coleman, a friend of Wilson, wrote that the appointment occurred Monday morning, when it appeared "that Lockett had no counsel [at arraignment]." This assertion, however, is disputed by quotes from the attorneys contained in the *Lexington Leader* Sunday edition, February 8, 1920. There, it was reported that "Lockett's attorneys, Colonel Samuel M. Wilson and George

R. Hunt, were in Frankfort Saturday in conference with [the accused], but they did not say what plea he will enter Monday."

I will defer to these quotes of able counsel in order to assess factual accuracy. As the trial was orchestrated, it is altogether likely that Judge Kerr at least warned Hunt and Wilson of their forthcoming appointments. It is probable that the decision not to announce which way Lockett would plead was to maintain silence on the part of Lockett. An announced plea in advance of either guilty or not guilty could have no other result but to make the situation more tumultuous.

These capable attorneys rose when Judge Kerr turned his attention to their table to determine the defense's readiness to proceed. George R. Hunt responded that "as a matter of form he would file a demurrer, but that the indictment was all right," according to the *Lexington Leader's* afternoon printing on Monday, February 9.

A demurrer was filed in the record on February 9, 1920. Signed by both Hunt and Wilson, the one-line pleading is all that appears in the entire court record on behalf of Will Lockett. It reads, "Defendant demurs to the Indictment for the want of legal sufficiency." As the trial was prepared to proceed, Will Lockett was brought into the courtroom from his holding cell and "there was a profound silence [in the courtroom] as he walked forth."

Lockett stood, shackled, with his head bowed as the deputy court clerk, George DeLong, read the 101-word indictment to formally charge the accused with the murder of Geneva Hardman. He was flanked on either side by his defense attorneys; four deputy sheriffs stood behind the three men.

Judge Kerr then inquired of the defendant, "Guilty or not guilty?" Lockett murmured a response. The defendant's response was "inaudible" according to reports. But George DeLong announced what he had heard: "Defendant pleads guilty, your Honor."

As previously noted, a guilty plea alters the dynamics at trial, because the burden no longer rests upon the commonwealth to prove guilt beyond a reasonable doubt. In pleading guilty, a defendant cedes his own guilt in the case. The remaining issue becomes one of punishment: would Will Lockett spend the remainder of his life behind bars, or would he be sentenced to die? (A third scenario—that a lynch mob might still succeed—also had a strong degree of possibility.)

The commonwealth called only one witness to the stand. It was the storekeeper from the South Elkhorn neighborhood, Claude B. Elkin. Elkin testified that he had been among those who had discovered Geneva's lifeless body lying in the cornfield. The bloodied stone with which she had been killed was identified by Elkin and admitted into evidence. With this evidence and the admission of guilt by the accused, the commonwealth rested.

A reporter from the *Lexington Leader* observed Will Lockett's demeanor and appearance during these proceedings. Lockett wore a "dark suit and a white soft collar" and "sat with closed eyes and with his right hand resting on his face" during nearly the entirety of the proceedings against him.

Attorney Samuel Wilson rose next. He did not rise to offer a defense on behalf of his client, but rather to ask only for mercy. It was all that was left for defense counsel after a plea of guilty. The following statement, read by Wilson, was signed by Will Lockett himself, though its authorship almost certainly belonged to the defense counsel.

I have plead [sic] guilty and have no defense to make to the charge against me. My fate is in your hands and I throw myself on the mercy of the court and jury.

I am sorry that I did it. I was sorry the minute after the deed was done and I don't know why I did it. I would give anything to bring the little girl back to life and undo the wrongs I have done.

I am 33 years of age. I was born in Henderson, Ky. My father and mother are dead and I have no blood kin that I know of. I have had very little education. Most of my life has been spent in farm labor.

I have never been tried in court for any offense except misdemeanors and I was never court martialed while in the army.

My wife died about a month ago and this has been on my mind.

I was in the military service for eleven months, all of the time at Camp Taylor near Louisville. I was first in the Pioneer Infantry and was afterwards transferred to the quartermaster's department and worked as a teamster about the camp. Lieutenant Fowler, a white officer, was my last commander. I was honorably discharged at Camp Taylor in May 1919. I submit my discharge certificate with this statement.

While at Camp Taylor, I was treated at one of the regimental infirmaries for disease. I have had this disease for ten or fifteen years. It may be this had something to do with the act I have committed. This disease and my ignorance are all I have to offer in explanation or extenuation of what I have done. I don't know why I did it.

It has been explained to me that the punishment for murder is death or confinement in the penitentiary for life, in the discretion of the jury. All I have to ask of the jury is this, that if you gentlemen of the jury can find it in your hearts and conscience to be merciful to me, that you will spare my life and not impose the death penalty, but send me to the penitentiary for life.

Samuel M. Wilson, one of Lockett's attorneys, in 1918 wearing his reserves uniform. *University of Kentucky Libraries.*

This is all I have to ask. I do not say that I deserve any mercy at your
hands, but, gentlemen of the jury, as you hope for mercy yourselves, I ask
you if you can be merciful to me?
     I have asked the lawyers appointed to defend me to read this statement
for me.
     (Signed) Will Lockett
     Witnessed: (signed) Gus Rogers, Huston Long

The statement offers some insight into Will Lockett's background. It is not, however, so much what is said but, rather, the flow and style of the statement that stands out. Such an eloquent statement—from someone with admittedly "very little education"—supports the argument that attorneys Hunt and Wilson wrote the statement on the weekend preceding the trial in Frankfort with their client. There, the two attorneys learned their client's story and strategized a defense. At a minimum, they planned to mitigate the punishment to be exacted. Another supportive fact for this theory was the signature of Gus Rogers. Rogers was the deputy warden of the reformatory at Frankfort where Lockett was held pending trial; Lockett and his attorneys must have been there when the statement was written in order that Rogers might serve as one of the witnesses to Lockett's signing of the statement. It is also clear that Will Lockett did not write this statement himself; more likely, it was written by defense counsel in that final effort to mitigate damages against their client. Neither the statement itself, nor Lockett's discharge certificate, appear in the archived court records.

A factual statement of Lockett's recent past may have been included to create a degree of sympathy in his favor on the part of the jury. That fact was the death of his wife a month or so earlier. It is a true detail confirmed by historical records and was not simply a ruse on the part of Lockett. The *Lexington Leader* reported on January 6, less than a month before Geneva's death, that "Katie Lockett died on the farm of O.F. Troutman, Monday afternoon. She leaves a husband, Will Lockett." Katie Gibbs and Will Lockett were married in 1914.

As Samuel Wilson read the statement, the sounds from the mob outside the courthouse grew louder. He was offering this statement at 9:28 a.m., when the sounds of gunfire outside reverberated in the ears of those in the courtroom. All jumped to their feet, panicked.

The electric energy outside the courthouse must have been felt inside, almost as if the stone walls of the building itself were being pressed upon from the outside. Lockett, ordinarily revealing no emotion during the morning's events, severely altered his expression with the eruption of gunfire. His eyes opened wide, and, according to the *Leader*, he "appeared frightened, but said nothing." Order was quickly restored inside the courtroom by the sheriff's deputies as they commanded all to sit down.

Attorney Samuel Wilson concluded his statement asking that his client might find mercy. When he had concluded, John Allen offered a brief statement on behalf of the commonwealth: "In all the history of crime none has been worse than committed by this defendant. In the name of the family of the slain child and of civilization, I ask you to act and sentence the defendant to death." Then, Allen added a final sentence that casts a pall upon the entire proceeding: "If you like, you may return the verdict without leaving the box."

The rush to complete the fatalistic trial with urgency was clear. The eruption of gunfire outside the building must have affected the emotions of those inside. And such a rush might satisfy the masses outside; the certainty of justice might satisfy the crowd's hunger for revenge for the death of Geneva Hardman. And, perhaps, the city of Lexington might be able to return to its routine existence. Judge Kerr and other local officials did, by all accounts, attempt to keep some semblance of judicial normalcy in the matter of *Commonwealth v. Lockett*.

But if all sought that semblance of justice, perhaps more could have been done to follow a more traditional trial. If the goal was to take action to mitigate the labeling of the local judiciary as a kangaroo court, then such normalcy is essential. With the defendant's confession, a trial needn't drag on. And quick it was. After the two sides had made their cases, the jury needed only to determine Lockett's sentence. So why would the jury remain in their box to deliberate sentencing in front of a room full of spectators? Why not return them to a deliberation room, as was customary?

Allen's suggestion that the jury remain in the box frustrated the legitimacy of the trial. Through the lens of our modern judicial system, the entire investigation and prosecution of the crime was tainted.

But we must, at the same time, consider the mood of the courtroom: the sound of gunfire had erupted outside, and those inside were panicked. A fatalistic perspective at the possible outcomes of continuing the trial based on these external factors would not change the end result: likely death for Lockett or, alternatively but less likely, a life sentence. Judge Kerr faced the option of declaring a mistrial and thus restarting the entire proceeding or continuing the sentencing phase to another date. The delay caused by a mistrial or continuance would not change Lockett's fate, but it likely could have further incited a city that demanded either Lockett or judicial expediency. It received the latter. Perhaps Judge Kerr did adhere to Lincoln's fatalistic belief system after all.

Judge Kerr opted to follow Colonel Allen's suggestion to permit the jurors to return their verdict without leaving their seats. He gave the jury its charge: "Gentlemen of the jury, you are directed to find the defendant guilty of murder and fix his punishment at life imprisonment in the penitentiary, or death, in your discretion."

The jury returned a death sentence at 9:40 a.m. Coleman's account suggests that at the moment the sentence was signed by the jury foreman, the gunfire outside erupted. But this does not comport with the other reported timelines. After being handed the sentence, Judge Charles Kerr advised those assembled of the jury's sentence. He went on to then speak directly to the condemned: "On the morning of March 11 before dawn you will meet death by the method provided by law. And may the God of all mercy have mercy on your soul."

Will Lockett would be electrocuted in Eddyville, Kentucky, on March 11, 1920.

FRIENDS KNOWN AND UNKNOWN FRIENDS

In the days and weeks that followed Geneva's death, expressions of grief and mourning were sent to her mother, Emma Hardman, at her home on Rural Route 8, Harrodsburg Pike. Some of the correspondence was delivered from those who knew Geneva, her siblings, or her mother. These friends known to the Hardman family sent heartfelt wishes and condolences, offering whatever aid they could do a grieving mother and family. Other letters from great distances also offered condolences of varying degrees of sincerity. Press accounts of Geneva's murder and Will Lockett's trial were carried via the wire services, and stories printed about the tragedy appeared nationally. It is difficult to see how the tone of certain of those expressions sent from "unknown friends" could have aided the heart of a grieving mother.

Yet Emma saved many, if not all, of the letters, notes, and cards she received from those she knew and those sent by people who would have learned of Geneva's tragic death through newsprint that carried the story across the nation. And the family keeps these family treasures still.

As is customary today, many floral arrangements were sent to the Hardman home. Each bore a small card embossed with the florist's name, JOHN A. KELLER CO., MAIN ST. OPP. PHOENIX HOTEL, and the name of the sending party penciled on its face. The flowers sent "from Joe's and Hugh's schoolmates" would have come from students about Geneva's age attending another school in Fayette County. (Joe and Hugh were Geneva's nephews, the sons of her older brother Tupper.)

One affectionate three-page letter was written by Geneva's aunt, Bettie Patterson of Winchester, in mid-March to her sister-in-law:

Winchester, Ky. Route 1. March 15 1920.

Dear Emma & Loved ones All,

How are you getting along! Oh how my heart gives out to you. think of you day and night & pray that you can trust God, in this terrible sorrow. I never had anything to hurt me so seemed like I couldn't live through it then when I think of you all [I] know we just have to. Emma you will have to be brave and live for your place couldn't be filled....

I will hope to see you and hear from you soon. [I] will not write more now, [I] am not sure about your Address, if you get this please answer.

Affectionately, Bettie S. Patterson

Aunt Bettie's letter opened with expressions of mourning and followed with much about family and neighbors. It seems that the sisters-in-law were not in regular communication, and such tragedy seemed to draw more correspondence from those who did not know the Hardman family than from those who did.

In one letter, sent from Mrs. Alfred (Mayme) Wiemann of Aylesford Place in Lexington, Kentucky, on the sixteenth of February, succinctly expressed the empathy "one mother does for another."

Mrs. Emma Hardman and family
Dear Friends,

First a line to express my heartfelt sympathy to you in your hour of great sorrow, I feel for you as one mother does for another, it is always painful to give our loved ones up, but these circumstances make it doubly hard.

You and your family have shown a true Christian spirit and I know God in his love will give you that comfort which only He can give. With deepest sympathy.

Sincerely,
Mrs. Alfred Wiemann
404 Aylesford Place

The reference to "true Christian spirit" likely was toward Tupper Hardman's public call on behalf of his family. It was a call for peace surrounding the trial and the desire that justice be allowed to prevail. Newspapers carried Tupper's statement, and many commented on the peaceful restraint encouraged and felt by the family.

Another mother expressed condolence and sympathized with Emma Hardman on the basis that she, too, had lost "six lovely children [her]self, two of them died within two weeks of each other." This letter, from Mrs. A.L. Plummer of Providence, Rhode Island, was typewritten save a few scrawled revisions. It was clear that Plummer was sending a form letter. The letter received by widow Emma Hardman was addressed to "Mr. and Mrs. Hardman," with only the family surname being penned by Plummer. The envelope was similarly addressed, with additions as follows:

Mr. and Mrs. Hardman
(Parents of little Geneva Hardman
who was murdered by negro Lockett)
c/o Lafayette [sic] *County Court House*
Lexington, Ky.

The postmaster crossed out the line relating to the courthouse and wrote "Harrodsburg Pike" to ensure a proper delivery of Plummer's form letter. We might never know how many of these letters were mailed by sixty-nine-year-old Agnes Plummer during her life. Perhaps her letter-writing campaign aided her in recovering from the grief she no doubt experienced in burying six of her own children. Or perhaps it was a spiritual mission whereby she sought out those nationwide to encourage that they might "Go to Him, our Redeemer for consolation." She further wrote to "Mr. and Mrs. Hardman" that Jesus would carry "you through the ordeal and bring you at last to your loved one gone to everlasting joy to be forever at rest."

The envelope from Mrs. Plummer of Providence, Rhode Island, to "Mr. and Mrs" Hardman. *Hardman/McGregor family collection.*

Some eight years earlier, Delilah Barham received a letter from Plummer. That letter, copied at length in a book by Nita Gould titled *Remembering Ella* about the 1912 murder in northwest Arkansas of an eighteen-year-old woman, was identical to the letter addressed to "Mr. and Mrs." Hardman in 1920. Some of Plummer's "heartfelt sympathy" was lost by her use of the typed form letter, which crossed out in pen any typewritten masculine identity of the victim. For example, a sentence from the letter from Plummer to Hardman read as follows: "And if you would but believe and be able to realize that if you could see your beloved ~~son~~ *daughter* in that supremely happy state of existence, you would not wish ~~him~~ *her* on the earth again," where the italicized words were penciled in above the marked-out masculine terms. Plummer also utilized the phrase "safe in the arms of Jesus," repeated in several of the letters from "unknown friends."

It is not known how Emma Hardman reacted to these letters, though she did keep each of them. Members of the Hardman family, a century on, know that whatever consolation the reference might offer pales in comparison to what would have been Emma's desire to have her little Geneva safe in her arms.

Members of the family today gravitate to the words written by Mr. and Mrs. E.C. Grinstead of Eureka Springs, Arkansas. The Grinstead letter reminds this author of the infamous letter purported to have been written

Feb. 11 th '20.

Mr. & Mrs. *Hardman*:

Having read of the awful catastrophe which has brought such
an affliction upon you, I desire to extend my heartfelt sympathy
to you. I have lost six lovely children myself, two of them died
within two weeks of each other. And I wish to say to you: Do not
think of your darling child as dead within the grave, but think of
the sweet living spirit now in the care of our Lord in glory.
"Safe in the arms of Jesus." And if you would but believe and be
able to realize that if you could see your beloved *one* in that
supremely happy state of existence, you would not wish *him* on the
earth again; and she would not want to come back, but has entered
into that higher life, awaiting your coming also. Let this comfort
you, and bring you nearer to our Saviour who has suffered and died
upon the cross for us, that if we will but believe in Him, we
shall be also where He has gone to prepare a place for us; and
where we will be reunited with the loved ones gone before, never
to part again.

"By grace we are saved through faith." This life is but
like a dream compared with that eternal blessed life to come. And
you do not know how much sorrow and tribulation your dear child
may have been spared by having been transferred from this world
wherein is so much woe, to that blissful home where there is no
more sorrow, suffering and death and no more tears for they will
all be wiped away, when once we shall be counted worthy to enter
into that heavenly home and haven of rest to be with the loved
ones gone before, never more to separate. Only believe in the
Saviour and in his precious promises, for He is faithful that
promised, and is ever ready and willing to receive and save us.

Read St. John 14th chapter: It is a comforting one. Go to
Him, our Redeemer for consolation. He will carry you through the
ordeal and bring you at last to your loved one gone to everlasting
joy to be forever at rest, happy and blest. Only believe in the
Saviour trustingly and He will comfort and bless you. Try to become reconciled and look hopefully forward for there is light not
darkness ahead, and this may work for you "a far more exceeding
and eternal weight of glory."

"Through much tribulation ye shall enter into the Kingdom
of Heaven."

                    Yours in sincere sympathy,
                    MRS. A. L. PLUMMER,
                    Providence, R. I.

The form letter from Agnes Plummer of Providence, Rhode Island, dated February 11, 1920. *Hardman/McGregor family collection.*

by President Lincoln to Mrs. Lydia Parker Bixby. Mrs. Bixby was a widow living Boston, Massachusetts, who was believed to have lost her five sons in the Civil War. Lincoln's letter to her, known for its sincere brevity, has been considered, along with the Gettysburg Address and his Second Inaugural Address, among his most exceptional written works. Wrote Mrs. Grinstead:

Feb. 8, 1920

Mrs. Emma Hardman,

My dear Mrs. Hardman: Received a letter from sister last night containing news of your terrible bereavement. I haven't words to express my feelings as I read the letter. It is terrible, terrible. We extend our deepest sympathy and wish you to know that we are remembering you in our prayers.
    May the dear God comfort, sustain and bless you as he alone can.

Sincerely,
Mr. & Mrs. E.C. Grinstead

The word *sister* as used in the Grinstead letter suggested a connection among the Grinsteads and the Hardmans. It turns out that Mrs. Grinstead's maiden name was Maude Snowden and that she was born in Clark County. The U.S. Census of 1900 identifies then eighteen-year-old Maude as living with her parents and siblings. The Snowden family lived *next door* to Ollie Hardman. Known friends from afar were reaching out to console their grieving acquaintance or friend who had so tragically lost her daughter.

The family collection of correspondence received by Emma Hardman includes postmarks from the mentioned Arkansas and Rhode Island locales, as well as from Detroit, Michigan, and several from various Kentucky communities.

In addition to the letters, both Geneva's school and the family's church offered resolutions of sympathy. Although her family had moved to South Elkhorn only in March of the previous year, Geneva and her family had become cherished members of the community.

The principal/schoolteacher, Anne S. Young, along with three of Geneva's classmates, offered this resolution on behalf of the school that Geneva attended:

> *Be it resolved that we, the teacher and pupils of the South Elkhorn school on account of the great sorrow we have sustained and the loss we have experienced in the death of our dear little pupil and school mate Geneva Hardman, express our heartfelt sympathy to the bereaved mother, sisters and brothers in their unconsolable [sic] grief, with the assurance that her memory will always be cherished with fond regard by her neighborhood and school.*

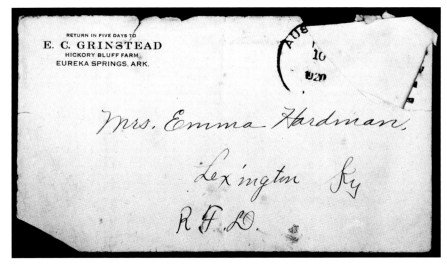

Top: An envelope postmarked Detroit, Michigan, addressed to Geneva's mother, Emma Hardman. *Hardman/McGregor family collection.*

Bottom: An envelope from Mr. and Mrs. Grinstead of Eureka Springs, Arkansas, to Geneva's mother. *Hardman/McGregor family collection.*

Be it further resolved that we express our appreciation of our association with Geneva, who was a child of unusual ability, ambitious to stand at the head of her classes and thereby creating a good natured rivalry among the other ambitious members of her class. Mirthful, cheerful, winsome and sweet with a smiling countenance illumined from the white soul within this child with such charming personality made a place for herself in the hearts of all who knew her.

With the assurance that the whole neighborhood mourns her loss and that her vacant seat in the school room will be a sweet memory in the hearts of her teacher and school mates who have loved and lost her be it further resolved that a copy of these resolutions be sent to the bereaved family.

[Signed] Mrs. Anne S. Young
Beatrice Stewart
Jewell Bunnell
Hazel Christian

The congregation of the church the Hardman family attended, and the site of Geneva's funeral, offered its own resolution, which is recorded in the church minutes:

Resolutions passed by the South Elkhorn Christian Church, Sunday, Febr'y 15th 1920

Whereas, in the death of Geneva Hardman there has come to her Mother and Family an indescribable sorrow, and

Whereas, Geneva was a faithful and highly respected pupil of the public school of this community and also of the Sunday School of this church

Be it Resolved by the people of the community of South Elkhorn assembled for worship in the South Elkhorn Christian Church:

First—That we express our most profound sympathy to Mrs. Hardman and Family in their bereavement.

Second—That we express our appreciation of the fine qualities of girlhood exemplified by Geneva in her life in the public school, the Sunday School, and in the community.

Third—That a copy of these Resolutions be sent to Mrs. Hardman & Family.

The resolutions passed by Geneva Hardman's church on Sunday, February 15, 1920, remembering her as they appear in the church's minutes. *South Elkhorn Christian Church.*

Whether from those who knew Geneva Hardman and her family, or whether from "unknown friends" who simply learned of the events that transpired from newspaper accounts, there was an outpouring of support expressed to Mrs. Hardman and family during their time of tragedy.

Geneva Hardman Is Laid to Rest

At the small Christian church where her family attended services, and where members of the family would continue to attend for decades more, a funeral service was held for little Geneva Hardman on the morning of Thursday, February 6, 1920—just two days after her brutal murder. The *Lexington Leader* reported that the church was "crowded" with friends of the young girl and her family.

The service was officiated by Reverend Elmer E. Snoddy, the senior minister of the church. Reverend Snoddy was also a theology professor at Transylvania College's College of the Bible. Snoddy was "armed with homely

Top: Reverend Elmer Ellsworth Snoddy was the senior minister of South Elkhorn Christian Church, where Geneva's family attended. He officiated at her funeral days after the murder. *South Elkhorn Christian Church*.

Bottom: These three headstones at Winchester Cemetery honor, from foreground to background, Geneva Hardman, her father, Rezin C. Hardman, and her mother, Emma Gillespie Hardman. *Author's collection*.

wisdom of the common people, with wit and a quick, germinal mind" and was "undoubtedly one of the most stimulating teachers ever to come to Lexington," according to Dwight Stevenson's centennial history of the Lexington Theological Seminary. During the service, Snoddy offered a tribute to Geneva's character and sweet disposition. Classmates of Geneva—Misses Jewell Bunnell, Alva Bunnell, Beatrice Stewart, Ella Stewart, Annie Hoskins and Iva Hoskins—served as pallbearers.

Following the service at South Elkhorn, a procession of about forty vehicles proceeded to a graveside service at the Winchester Cemetery conducted by Dr. G.W. Banks of Winchester's First Baptist Church. There in the Winchester Cemetery, Geneva was laid to rest beside her father.

On Monday morning, the morning of the trial, the *Herald* provided additional information about Dr. Snoddy's remarks at the funeral. Apparently, it was at Geneva's funeral that it was announced from the pulpit that a "group from the neighborhood would be permitted to [witness] Lockett's execution when it takes place at Eddyville." These remarks by Reverend Snoddy were approved and encouraged by Judge Kerr and other local authorities. It was another statement on the inevitability that surrounded the trial and the fate of the accused. It was also not the only instance during this season of Lexington's history where local authorities directed the content of a Sunday sermon.

Part Four

THE SECOND BATTLE OF LEXINGTON

T he shots that had been fired at 9:28 a.m. on the morning of February
9, 1920, were not merely warning shots. Some thought them to
be those of a machine gun rattling off rounds into the mob that
sought entrance into the old courthouse "to rob the law of its victim." Final
reports indicated that the machine gun saw little to no use, while soldiers
firing above the crowd with automatic weapons caused the reverberating
sounds. Ultimately, neither the gauge of the bullets nor the type of firearm
discharged altered the outcome. The afternoon *Lexington Leader*'s afternoon
headline read: "Four Persons Lose Their Lives When Attempt Made to
Storm Court House." In the newspaper the following morning, citizens
learned that the initial fatality list was an undercount. Although five killed
had been immediately reported, a sixth would die from injuries sustained.
And still, another score suffered.

The crowd largely respected the steel cables that served as a waist-high
barrier around the courthouse. One man elbowed his way toward the front
of the crowd carrying a rope; he was spotted by a Fayette County sheriff's
deputy. The deputy left his post on the sidewalk and descended into the
crowd to recover the rope. A fistfight ensued, but the deputy emerged from
the crowd with two men in custody.

As the deputy returned under the steel cables, some in the mob followed.
Authorities ordered the surging crowd to reverse course, but their efforts
failed. Some members of the crowd began surging past the cables and
toward the front stairs of the courthouse. One man interviewed by the

A machine gunner smiles for the camera from an elevated platform around the Main Street side of the Fayette County Courthouse. *J. Winston Coleman Photo Collection, Transylvania University Library*.

Guardsmen point their guns eastward down Main Street away from the courthouse. The clock in the left of the photo outside of Skuller's jewelry and pawnshop is in its original location. The clock was first put up in 1911. *Kentucky National Guard eMuseum*.

Lexington Leader offered his account of an increasingly dense crowd: "The crowd was getting denser and denser, and they started shoving. Before we knew what had happened we were pushed under the wire rope and were being pushed up the steps."

By most accounts, the first shot was fired by General Deweese either as a warning shot to those in the crowd thrusting forward to get back or as a signal to his men to open fire. A statement made by him after the shooting indicates that it was a signal of action to his own troops but that he had "averted" the shooting as "long as possible."

Although the machine gun was not "put into regular action," rumors of its widespread use abounded as those assembled saw scores of men dropping in the melee. It was thought that the death toll would far exceed the number that ultimately resulted. It was one of several rumors that spread following the shooting. The reports of men dropping were likely a misunderstanding of the instinctual reaction to the source of gunfire: drop to the ground.

SHAKE YOUR FISTS AND YELL

One of the most popular rumors, memorialized in Coleman's *Death at the Court-House*, was that a newsreel cameraman had excited the already electric crowd by riling them up. Allegedly, the cameraman yelled to those nearby to "shake your fists and yell." This added fire to the "highly charged atmosphere." Some have discounted this theory on the basis that newsreels were not yet popular and that there was no evidence of the existence of such a newsreel. The first objection to the theory is false; newsreels began during the decade before the Lockett trial. And the second argument against it is refuted by advertisements carried in newspapers from other communities. Even the *Lexington Herald* has a short reference to the existence of such motion pictures. So the newsreels did, in fact, exist. Yet today, the reels may exist in a lost archive or could be damaged and destroyed.

The *Danville Advocate* carried an advertisement in March 1920 that Stout's Theatre would have the added newsreel attraction of "The Moving Pictures of the Riots in Lexington Kentucky when the Mob Wanted to Lynch Will Lockett." An editorial by "W.S.S." immediately below the advertisement encouraged readers not to miss the show so that they might see the "great mob…after Will Lockett." At the Columbia Theatre in Portsmouth, Ohio, a one-night special featuring the newsreels was shown. The advertisement running in the *Portsmouth Daily Times* on February 28, 1920, read that "Pathe News secured exclusive pictures of the actual storming of the county courthouse by the mob during the recent mob riots at Lexington, Ky." and that theaters in that Ohio River community would show the reels.

On Saturday, February 14, a private showing of the riot films taken by Jack Dadswell was given to Major R.P. Smith, who served as the personal adjutant to General Francis C. Marshall. Also present at the showing were Captain Pete Rodes and Sheriff J. Waller Rodes. The viewing occurred in the University of Kentucky's projection room. The *Herald* wrote that the showing would "probably be the last ever given in Lexington." The reels were prohibited from being shown in Lexington by order of Mayor Thomas C. Bradley. Both the Strand and Ben Ali theaters agreed to this prohibition. The private viewing was in order to assess whether or not the film had value for the grand jury in making any determination on whether or not to prosecute any of those in the mob. After the viewing, it was determined that it did not.

Although the moving pictures may not have provided evidence sufficient for a court of law, the images certainly carry historic significance. And the mere existence of them lends support to the anecdotal story that Dadswell—or perhaps some other individual—did encourage the crowd toward more excitement.

Perhaps the reason why the newsreel theory has been discounted is the lack of awareness of these short advertisements and articles. Historian John D. Wright Jr., however, conclusively wrote that the cameraman's request of the crowd is what "sparked the attack." It is said that the few pumping their fists and yelling emboldened those already pressing against and perhaps passing the restraining cable wire. It is a most plausible theory and one that is, at least partially, supported by the existence of newsreels.

JUDGE BULLOCK'S INVOLVEMENT

Another widely circulated rumor was entirely false. A soldier taking aim on the crowd from the office of Fayette County judge-executive Frank Bullock prompted the rumor that Judge Bullock himself had fired some shots during the morning volley; some even suggested that the first shot was fired by Bullock. Judge Bullock, however, was in the courtroom during the entirety of the trial. General Deweese came to the defense of Bullock as these rumors grew. "A man from the military organization" stationed at the window of Judge Bullock's office followed the general's orders when he fired his weapon, as it "became necessary to repel the mob from the courthouse." Deweese knew "absolutely that [Bullock] had nothing to do with the shooting."

Judge Bullock issued his own statement concerning this rumor, which was widespread in the community. As a result of the rumor, threats were made against his life. Bullock's statement, carried in the next editions of each of the local daily newspapers, described the rumor as "entirely false." From the courtroom, it was the sound of the gunshots that first caused him to realize the trouble that had begun outside. When martial law was later declared, this rumor remained one of the top priorities for the military governor because of the threats against Bullock's life. Military communications from Lexington to the intelligence officer of the U.S. Army's Central Command in Chicago during the two-week existence of martial law in the city include three references to threats against Judge Bullock. There are also references to threats being made against Deputy Sheriff Walter Stivers and against the tobacco warehouses owned by Sheriff Rodes.

MAYHEM

With members of the mob storming up the exterior front stairs of the old courthouse and approaching the doors facing Main Street, soldiers and sheriff's deputies emerged from the courthouse with their rifles and shotguns raised. The warning shot of General Deweese was the cue to these guardsmen to fire on the citizens of Fayette County. In one burst, those in the mob pressing upon the steps were halted and repelled. Others, however, returned fire, and it is estimated that some fifty shots were fired in the direction of the courthouse. In total, there were twenty-nine casualties, including six fatalities. This number, however, does not begin to account for those whose unidentified injuries were treated in drugstores or at home after either being struck with buckshot or being knocked down in the melee.

Most of the shots fired at those defending the courthouse missed. Evidence of the gunfire was visible until recently in the façade of and on the steps to the old courthouse. Bullet holes and chipped masonry were repaired during the renovations to the courthouse completed in 2018. Bullets otherwise ricocheted throughout the square: "Several of the shots passed thru the

The altercation between local authorities and the mob. *J. Winston Coleman Photo Collection, Transylvania University Library.*

crowd and crashed thru the plate-glass windows on the opposite side of the street." Store windows were shattered.

All of the shots were fired within ten seconds, but the damage was complete. The rumor against Judge Bullock found "ready believers" in a mob that sought justice not only against Lockett but also those who had defended him. Quickly, several in the mob descended on local pawnshops in search of procuring additional firearms to aid in their cause.

Only two pawnshops were open. Stores owned by Harry Skuller and Joe Rosenberg—names that would remain significant in Lexington for decades to come—were quickly filled with those simultaneously seeking revenge and protection. According to Skuller, promises were made to return the weapons. He handed over nearly fifty revolvers from his stock; Joe Rosenberg did the same thing for the "determined" mob. Military intelligence reports indicate that the two may have inflated their separate inventories and that some fifty or sixty pistols, in total, were removed from the pawnshops. By Friday, only seven of the "borrowed" revolvers were returned to Rosenberg's store. Yet both Skuller and Rosenberg were confident that the other firearms would soon be returned. Separate accounts indicated multiple attempts to break into the armory at the University of Kentucky. Another rumor suggested that fifteen hundred men from the mountains of eastern Kentucky were on their way to Lexington.

The looting of pawnshops and hardware stores in search of additional weapons indicates that the energy of the mob had not fully subsided. Perhaps these actions also led authorities to request outside help.

Some vehemently defended the actions of the mob and opposed even the use of the word. In what would be seen today as an attempt to revise history, a reader of the *Leader* suggested to the newspaper that the use of the word *mob* was entirely inappropriate. In the judgment of this unnamed reader, the term *indignant citizens* would be more accurate. Another, a physician, wrote a letter to the newspaper making a similar demand. To support the newspaper's use of the word, the *Leader* responded under the caption "What is a mob?" by quoting Webster: a mob is "a disorderly element of the populace."

Curiously, even the Kentucky legislature had defined a "mob" by statute, although that statute would not go into effect until after February 1920. That provision defined a mob as "any number of persons more than three, assembled for the purpose of doing violence, injury to, or lynching any person in custody of any peace officer or jailer in the commonwealth."

Under any definition, the group that sought to capture Will Lockett was a "disorderly element of the populace." And although we cannot know the minds of those who charged toward the courthouse, the circumstances suggest that their intent was to lynch Lockett.

THE RIOT VICTIMS

The first casualty from the mob violence, and the guardsmen's response to it, was William Hiram Ethington of Versailles, Kentucky. He was thirty-three. Ethington's father, J.H. Ethington, had also been at the scene. The father's letter to the editor of the newspaper expressed appreciation to those in law enforcement who attempted to keep the peace, but he expressed his anger toward the soldiers who discharged weapons from the upper floors of the courthouse. Ethington's anger truly was focused on the soldier who had occupied the window of Judge Bullock's second-floor office in the courthouse. His was not an uncommon emotion felt by many in the community who felt that lives would have been saved and a larger crisis averted had Lockett simply been turned over to the mob. Such a result would not have been unprecedented. In at least three similar occasions in Kentucky in the 1910s, a jailer released his prisoner to a lynch mob.

The first to die, Ethington was not even taken to the hospital. Instead, he passed at the office of Dr. Heizer in the Fayette National Bank Building. City ambulances transported the remainder of the wounded, including those who would soon perish, to St. Joseph Hospital. Those who died were generally transported to the "undertaking establishment" owned by John Milward.

James Masengale, a thirty-eight-year-old brickmason living in Lexington's Irishtown neighborhood, died two days after the riots from "gunshot wounds inflicted by authorities during riot," according to his death certificate. The death certificates of the other victims of the riot bore similar, if not identical, causes of death. Since the morning of the riot, Masengale had languished from his wound at St. Joseph Hospital. He left behind a widow to care for their three children, all under the age of seven. On the day Masengale died, the other five who were killed at the riot were buried. John Van Thomas and William Ethington, both of Versailles, are buried in Versailles; the other four riot victims are buried at the Lexington Cemetery.

Benjamin F. Carrier was a Prudential Insurance agent who lived on Carlisle Avenue. Reverend J.E. Wilson of the Arlington Christian Church stated at Carrier's funeral that Carrier was "not in favor of mob rule and had cautioned young men of his community against taking any part in the violence." Reverend Wilson further concluded that, although Carrier was one of the victims of the riot, he "was not a member of the mob…but was a bystander during the rioting." The *Herald* also came to Carrier's defense, stating that he had been "vindicated of any participation in the activities of the mob." Wilson, along with Reverend Mark Collis of Broadway Christian Church, conducted the funeral at the home of Carrier's bereaved father, John, on Wednesday afternoon.

Earlier in the morning, Reverend Collis also conducted the 10:00 a.m. funeral for John M. Rogers. Rogers, a Fayette County farmer, was sixty-six years old and lived along the Frankfort Pike. An hour later, another funeral was conducted at the cemetery. This one was for Major L.M. King, a retired farmer who resided on Winnie Street.

Those injured, however, made up over two-thirds of the total number of casualties. And to reiterate, the list of those twenty or so injured did not include the many more who were quickly released from drugstores or who treated their injuries via homemade remedies.

One of the injured outside the old Fayette County courthouse during the Second Battle of Lexington. *J. Winston Coleman Photo Collection, Transylvania University Library.*

One victim who suffered a non-life-threatening injury during the violence was J.W. Stansell, who was shot "once in the right hip and once in the left shoulder." He wrote a letter to the editor calling attention to the many who denied firing their weapons and the few who did. "Everybody says they didn't shoot," he wrote. "But if all those who did shoot would send me a dollar apiece I could pay my doctor's bills and feed my five little ones." Stansell, a veteran of the Spanish-American War, died in 1960 and is buried at Camp Nelson National Cemetery.

"Defenders of the courthouse" were also injured. Elmer Moore, a trooper with the national guard from Covington, was injured, having been struck in the abdomen by a bullet. Three Lexington Police Department patrolmen were shot. Patrolman Walter Franklin Ely received his injury in his right hand, but he was saved by a heavy bunch of keys that stopped a bullet to his chest. Patrolman John Caleb Clancy received an injury to his left arm that required amputation at the elbow. Patrolman John Cropper received a gunshot wound from his perch on the upper level of the courthouse entrance, where he had estimated the number of shots fired by the mob at fifty.

The remainder of the injuries were sustained by those in the mob. A nearly universal characteristic of those on the casualty list consisted in their being white males. Irma Cross, a twenty-one-year-old stenographer, was the only female injured in the riot. She, like Carrier, was merely an innocent bystander. The stationery shop where she worked was directly across from the courthouse. Curious, she watched the events unfolding across the street when a stray bullet broke the window of the shop and struck her calf.

Despite the casualties, General Deweese believed he took the correct course of action. "I'd do again just as I have done," he said. Lexington's police chief, Jere Reagan, echoed the general's comments by expressing sorrow at the loss of bloodshed but indicating that those injured had received "enough warning." He believed that discharging the weapons was of an "absolute necessity" given how certain members of the mob had rushed past the steel cables and up the steps of the courthouse. "I really believe that had the mob not been turned back, they would have broken into the courtroom," he said. Such a result might have rendered all efforts to protect both justice and the life of the accused futile.

Other groups and individuals also called for peace. Dr. P.D. Robinson of Lexington, Kentucky, wrote a letter to the editor of the *Leader* observing that the tragedy shocked "colored people" as much as others and called that justice might be both "swift and sure." The physician, a prominent member of the African American community, noted in his letter that "members of the Negro race gave evidence which led to [Lockett's] capture." The *Herald* carried comments from two other "colored civic organizations," the Civic League and the Ministers' Alliance, both of which also called for law and order to prevail. The former expressed gratitude that the "papers were thoughtful and kind enough to lay the crime to the individual and not a people."

An *Associated Press* wire report dated February 10 provides the text of a telegraph that had been sent to Governor Morrow by the National Association for the Advancement of Colored People. It read, "In commending your honorable action, the board [of the NAACP] expresses the view that you have set a worthy example to all governors and civil authorities everywhere, which, if followed, would relieve our country of the disgrace cast upon it when lynching mobs do their will in overriding law."

The National Association for the Advancement of Colored People celebrated the antilynching effort from its national offices. Writing in the NAACP's official publication, *The Crisis*, famed civil rights leader W.E.B. DuBois wrote of the events under the lasting caption "The Second Battle of Lexington":

How high shall we value human life?

In Massachusetts, in 1775, eight men were killed in the battle of Lexington. Was it worth while? The shot "was heard 'round the world!"

In Kentucky, in 1920, five men were killed in the second battle of Lexington. Was it worth while?

Already lynch law has cost America 3,000 lives, and mob law has taken ten times as many. If further bloody toll can be saved by five deaths, we have gotten off far more cheaply than we deserve.

DuBois's wish that the "bloody toll" of lynching would end at this second battle of Lexington was full of hope, yet mob law and lynching would sadly continue in both Kentucky and across the nation. It was also hard to find many in Lexington who would embrace DuBois's words. Although the sentiments in the community varied, the prevailing attitude was that the "mob was justifiable in its actions and in the best interest of society." This was the observation of Lieutenant Colonel Maddox in his daily summary of events to military intelligence on February 17. In his report, he wrote that "a large number of citizens honestly believe and openly maintain that Lockett's crime as so hedious [sic] a character as to place the criminal outside the protection and process of the law." Those holding these beliefs also believed that the punishments that could be exacted under the law were "wholly inadequate" and that the public's respect for the "laws of humanity" would better be upheld if "human brutes of the Lockett type" were dealt with in a manner so as to "inflict the greatest possible punishment on the criminal, and, at the same time, to express before the world some measure of the burning anger and indignation of an outraged community." Maddox concluded his report by observing that he did not believe these sentiments would quickly wane, but rather that it would be "many months, and perhaps years" until those holding these views would "cease to argue that the mob was right and the authorities wrong."

A NATIONAL RESPONSE

General Deweese and Chief Reagan were not alone in celebrating the role of the guardsmen, the deputies, the police, and all local officials in quelling the riot and repelling the mob from the courthouse. The *Lexington Herald* collected comments on the "affair" from newspapers both regional and across the country. Almost universally, the reporting newspapers celebrated the preservation of the cause of justice.

During the days and weeks preceding Geneva's murder and the Lockett trial, newspapers near and far carried stories of the Red Scare. In the summer of 1918, Russian czar Nicholas and his family were executed by Bolshevik rebels. Nine months later, a group formed in Moscow with the intent of the worldwide spread of communism—a movement that did gain momentum across the globe, including within the United States. Local newspapers like the *Herald* and the *Leader* lauded efforts to capture the "Reds" and celebrated that "Lexington stands out as one of the one-hundred-percent all-American cities." Lexingtonians believed their community was superior to other communities as the Red Scare was not seen as afflicting this community; this elitism was described as "smugness" by historian John D. Wright. In his works, he suggested that the blot of the Hardman murder and the ensuing mob scene showed Lexington's own flaws. It also became a new focus for newspapers.

The *Louisville Post* offered a "well done" congratulations to all those involved, from the local deputy sheriffs "on duty at the spot" up to Governor Morrow, describing the incident as one in which no "Kentuckian need be ashamed." Despite the rush toward justice that may have resulted in an incorrect man being sentenced to death, the "barbarous ritual of Judge Lynch" did not prevail.

The *Cincinnati Enquirer* attempted to tie the unruly mob to international events by suggesting that "the spirit of Bolshevism" was moving the mob in a "lawless and unwarranted manner." There was no evidence, however, to support the idea that such an influence was present in the mob. The Cincinnati newsmen drew the connection because of the widespread notion across the nation that expressions of lawlessness, whether in the form of a lynch mob or a striking labor union, indicated the presence of Bolshevik influence. The *Enquirer* concluded, however, that the spirit that prevailed was the "true spirit of Kentucky" found in the "dignified progress of justice." The *Eagle*, a newspaper published in Brooklyn, New York, similarly connected the Lexington mob with the International Workers of the World union and other "Red" influences.

The references to an influence of Bolshevism carried by the newspapers in Brooklyn and Cincinnati were not isolated concerns. Even General Marshall remarked on the subject by indicating how Lexington served as a "fine example against Bolshevism and lawlessness." But the military intelligence reports indicated that there was "no evidence of any foreigners in the mob." Any suggestion that there was such an influence was asserted solely for political gain.

The *Louisville Times* sympathized with those in the mob, citing the inherent "delays" in the judicial process, the risk of prisoner escape when being held, and unprosecuted crimes. None of those factors were present, however. As obtuse as we now view this editorial, it does help to understand the conflicting perspectives of 1920 Kentucky. Citing a more or less prevalent belief that "lynching is the punishment which fits the crime committed by Lockett; that lynching has a salutary effect through terrorizing those who might attack women," the Louisville paper stopped short of endorsing the mob's behavior. Instead, it merely rationalized it. The editorial did at least acknowledge that in the Lockett case, such a rationale was not even warranted. This was because the case against Lockett was "meted out as quickly as the simplest forms of law could be observed without turning the court into an agency for legalized lynching." It went on to call for Kentucky courts to more swiftly advance justice, as was done in the Lockett case: "the jury did its duty quickly; the Judge passed sentence promptly; and the Governor signed the death warrant immediately."

The editor of the *Nicholas News* in Carlisle, Kentucky, however, had a completely different take, believing that justice could have been better served, and tragedy avoided, had the venue of the trial been moved to another county. Although this alternative had been considered by Judge Kerr and Judge-Executive Bullock, the decision was intentionally made to keep the trial in Lexington.

Other Kentucky newspapers ran short editorials as well. Some were chosen by the *Herald's* editorial board for reprinting, including those from Shelbyville's *Shelby Record*, Mt. Sterling's *Sentinel-Democrat*, Lancaster's *Central Record*, Lawrenceburg's *Anderson News*, the *Jackson Times*, the *Hazard Herald*, the *Nicholasville Times*, Stanford's *Interior-Journal*, the Cynthiana *Democrat*, and the *Wilmore Enterprise*. "The slaughter of innocents…was one of those things that had to be," wrote the editors in Cynthiana. The *Hazard Herald* advised that Lexingtonians had "lost the right" to criticize those in eastern Kentucky "for this affair is worse than any mountain feud."

The editorial from the *Wilmore Enterprise* found the whole affair unnecessary because "the wretched brute" had been condemned to death "before the catastrophe occurred." A fatalistic take, indeed. Although the timeline was not accurate, the die had certainly been cast, and there was no doubt in anyone's mind how the trial would proceed. The unnecessary deaths of those in the mob, therefore, constituted (in the words from the

Nicholasville News' editorial) "one of the worst affairs which ever took place in the history of Kentucky."

The *Cincinnati Times-Star* concluded its editorial to describe the only affair that would have been worse than the events that did occur on February 9, 1920: if the mob had secured "Lockett's body and [soiled] the fair name of Kentucky with the ineradicable blot of a lynching."

In addition to the editorializing, the news of the mob spread via the Associated Press wire service across America. Those in Chicago, Washington, and New York awoke on February 10 to news of a riot in Lexington, Kentucky. Others, too, carried the news in Arizona, Arkansas, Wisconsin, Nebraska, and other states across the nation. Some of these newspapers would follow the story until Lockett was electrocuted a month later.

The *New York Times* began its coverage on February 10, the day after the Lockett trial. The front-page headline proclaimed: "Troops Kill Five in Kentucky Mob Out to Get Negro." That article took up a full front-page column that continued onto the second page. The story was continued the following day when the *Times* reported, on page 6, that Lockett had been removed from Lexington to Eddyville for execution. Finally, a third *New York Times* article related to these events ran on March 12, 1920, proclaiming on page twenty-five that "Will Lockett Is Executed; Kentucky Negro Pays Penalty for Murder of 10-Year-Old-Girl." It is evidence of the national interest in this story that the *Times* would run three pieces on the subject, albeit on decreasingly significant positions in the newsprint.

The tragedies that occurred in early February 1920 were good business for the newspapers, as the *Herald* proudly reported on the Wednesday morning just one week after Geneva's death: "Sale of Herald Tuesday Nears that of Monday." Monday sales were, of course, high, given the interest in the Lockett trial. But the trouble at the courthouse also caused an "unexpected demand for the Tuesday morning" edition, so much so that the regular Tuesday *Herald* printed almost as many copies as "the regular edition and all of the extra editions on Monday." The news captivated the community, probably more so than the all-important question of the health of the president. (President Woodrow Wilson's unknown location and health were of concern for the Republican-leaning papers but were all but ignored in those papers with editors and owners who favored Democratic politics. Wilson had, however, secretly suffered a major stroke in October 1919, and First Lady Edith Wilson largely ran the country.) Instead, the newsies urged potential readers to pick up their paper's latest edition.

It was, however, the *Lexington Herald* on the morning of February 10, 1920, that best captured the mood of the people of Lexington, under the headline "Lexington Mourns." A seven-paragraph editorial began by proclaiming that "Lexington is under a burden of grief. Her eyes are dim with tears, her heart is a town with sympathy for the families of those who mourn their loved ones, the victims of Monday's tragedy." The editorial also expressed Lexingtonians' shame that the "temple of justice was attacked while her officers of the law" were following the "mandate of the law." And the *Herald* lauded the swift justice that brought a death sentence to Will Lockett while simultaneously not turning him over to the mob that sought to lynch him. It concludes by expressing gratitude to those who "obeyed their oath of office."

UNDER MARTIAL LAW

The response to the mob riot was handled not just by guardsmen, local police, and deputy sheriffs. After the riot, federal assistance was requested to Lexington, as it was unclear whether the crowd was subdued or whether additional violence would arise. Their search for additional weaponry at local pawnshops suggests the latter. Almost immediately after the incident, Governor Morrow requested the presence of federal troops to Lexington from Camp Zachary Taylor, located just outside of Louisville.

Named after the former president who had spent several of his formative years growing up in Louisville, Camp Taylor had been established in 1917, just as America was entering into World War I. At its peak, the camp included some seventeen hundred buildings and housed over forty thousand troops. It would close in 1920, just a few months after the troops were ordered to action in nearby Lexington. When it closed, all of Camp Taylor's remaining installments and functions were transferred to nearby Camp Knox, which had been significantly enhanced in 1918. In 1932, Camp Knox became a permanent garrison and assumed its current moniker: Fort Knox. The orders to the Second Battalion were received by 10:00 a.m. A mere thirty minutes or so had lapsed since the shooting had begun.

Those in the mob remained unaware of the movement of any federal troops toward their location. "Reports were current that the leaders were biding their time," Coleman wrote of the scene in which those assembled simply were "waiting for darkness to shoot out the street lights, dynamite the building and overwhelm its defenders." Meanwhile, all commerce had dispersed from the usually bustling Main Street. As the hours wore on, the courthouse was "besieged by an unusually large number of armed men [displaying] an increasingly threatening attitude."

GENERAL FRANCIS MARSHALL

At 12:20 p.m., Brigadier General Francis C. Marshall of the Second Infantry Brigade, along with four hundred troops of the Provisional Riot Company of the Twenty-Eighth Infantry, left the Louisville and Nashville Railroad, or L&N, station in Louisville destined for Lexington. Minutes ahead of the special train carrying the troops was another scout train. The purpose of the scout train was to ensure that no bombs had been planted along the tracks. The scout train, if destroyed, would cause far fewer casualties than if something tragic were to happen to the troop train. Fortunately, no bombs had been placed along the tracks between Louisville and Lexington. Both trains arrived safely at their destination. The federal troops arrived a few

General Francis C. Marshall in France during World War I. He was named the military governor of Fayette County during martial law. *National Archives.*

hours later, at 3:15 p.m., deboarding on Water Street near its intersection with Mill Street. They were a short two blocks from the courthouse. Unlike the young guardsmen who had exchanged the earlier volleys of gunfire with the mob, the soldiers arriving were battle-hardened.

Military intelligence reports provided that the two squads were met by a "mob of several hundred men" as they disembarked from their train onto Water Street. According to these reports, the troops met "no resistance" from the "mob of approximately ten thousand," which had concentrated themselves around the courthouse.

The referenced intelligence reports provide a wealth of details about the mood in town during the duration of martial law as well as observations on the unrest that prompted it. The military intelligence reports are each addressed from the "Intelligence Officer, U.S. Troops, Lexington, Ky." to either the intelligence officer for the Central Department in Chicago,

Illinois, or to the Director of Military Intelligence, Washington, D.C. During the era between the two world wars, U.S. intelligence, specifically the army's Military Intelligence Division, largely focused on domestic activity. The Military Intelligence Division, or MID, was created during the First World War. After the war, domestic intelligence existed because of threats from both anarchist and communist groups that were perceived to threaten the rule of law. Military intelligence reports investigated race riots, labor strikes, and other uprisings with a particular eye toward any "foreign" influence. The reports relating to the military occupation of Lexington remained classified until 1986.

Pouring out of the L&N coaches they had ridden in, these soldiers, bayonets fixed, assembled in formation and marched north on Mill Street. A color guard flew the flag of the nation and led the troops as the "column executed a smart turn east onto Main Street and quickly bore down on the astounded mobsters." Their march from the train to the courthouse lasted eight minutes.

It took only five more minutes for the area around the courthouse to be cleared. Few in the mob raised more than a weak argument in the face of a rifle butt or bayonet. It was as "if by magic" that the federal troops were able

The American flag is positioned on the steps of the Fayette County Courthouse. Moments later, General Marshall declared martial law. *J. Winston Coleman Photo Collection, Transylvania University Library.*

to restore order in Lexington. General Marshall saw to it that the Stars and Stripes was planted on the courthouse lawn before proclaiming that the city of Lexington was being placed under martial law.

> WHEREAS a state of lawlessness exists in the County of Fayette, State of Kentucky, with which the State authorities are unable to cope, and;
>
> WHEREAS the Governor of the said State of Kentucky, has asked for the aid of the United States in restoring and maintaining order in the said County of Fayette;
>
> NOW, therefore, I, Brigadier General Francis C. Marshall, U.S. Army, commanding the United States troops in the said County, do hereby declare a state of MARTIAL LAW in the said County, do assume all functions, both civil and military in said County.
>
> All citizens are warned to respect and obey my orders and those of my subordinates.
>
> > F.C. Marshall,
> > Brigadier General United States Army
>
> Lexington, Ky., February 9, 1920.

General Marshall served during the First World War and was decorated for his valorous command of the Second Infantry Brigade, First Division, during the Battle of Meuse-Argonne. An 1890 graduate of West Point, Marshall would tragically die in a plane crash on the eastern slope of Japacha Peak just east of San Diego, California, in 1922. On board the deadly flight were a young pilot and General Marshall. The flight had originated in San Diego and was destined for Fort Huachuca, Arizona, where Marshall was scheduled to conduct a military inspection. Bad weather caused the biplane to return toward San Diego, and on the return flight it crashed into the mountainside, probably due to low visibility resulting from the poor weather conditions. Five months later, a rancher discovered wreckage along with the burned remains of the two veterans. A military entourage was brought to retrieve the bodies and wreckage, but the plane's engine block was too heavy to be transported down the mountain. It was built into a memorial to the two men who perished on what is today known as Airplane Ridge. Marshall's body was returned to, and is buried at, his alma mater, West Point.

In Lexington, the veteran leader from the Battle of Meuse-Argonne issued an order at 4:30 p.m. that any loiterers remaining in thirty minutes' time would be arrested. By the 5:00 o'clock hour, the mob was "entirely dispersed" and troops were in control of the downtown blocks surrounding the courthouse.

These initial 400 troops of the Twenty-Eighth Infantry were reinforced about 6:00 p.m. by another approximately 800 troops of the Twenty-Sixth Infantry. The total number of federal troops occupying Lexington during martial law peaked at approximately 1,200. (These rounded figures found in some sources overstate the precise numbers utilized by Coleman, "872 soldiers and 34 officers." The higher numbers likely include both the initial guardsmen, local authorities, and federal troops.)

The troops under the command of General Marshall consisted of provisional organizations from the Second Infantry Brigade, the Twenty-Sixth Infantry, the Twenty-Eighth Infantry, the Third Machine Gun Battalion, the First Infantry Brigade, the Sixteenth Infantry, the Eighteenth Infantry, the Second Machine Gun Battalion, the First Field Artillery Brigade, the Fifth Field Artillery, the Sixth Field Artillery, the Seventh Field

General Marshall reviews papers while standing along Main Street. A statue of John Hunt Morgan, a Confederate general during the Civil War, can be seen in the background. That statue was relocated to the Lexington Cemetery in 2018. *J. Winston Coleman Photo Collection, Transylvania University Library.*

An M1917 tank at Main Street and Cheapside. *Kentucky National Guard eMuseum.*

Artillery, the Second Field Signal Battalion, the First Sanitary Train, and the Motor Transport Corps.

Troops stationed here pitched tents on Stoll Field at the University of Kentucky. The area known as Stoll Field originally served as pastureland for cattle owned by the university's first president, James K. Patterson. A new sport, football, began to be played by students on these fields for three games in 1881. After a nine-year hiatus, the school fielded a team in 1891; the field was named Stoll Field after Richard C. Stoll in 1916. Later in 1920, plans were unveiled for a twenty-four-thousand-seat stadium to be constructed around the field of play. Stoll Field was situated at the northern edge of the college campus, which itself was to the south of town. Troops would have traveled approximately eight to ten blocks to arrive at the courthouse from their encampment.

Soldiers established outposts on the roads into Lexington, and the city was divided into four military zones. The first zone consisted of the University of Kentucky and its immediate vicinity. The second zone included each of the roads, including railroads, that led into and out of Lexington. The third zone was a core downtown area bounded by Church

Street to the north, Broadway to the west, Water Street to the south, and Limestone Street to the east. Finally, the fourth zone included the east end, a predominately African American sector of town. The fourth sector was preventative in the event that racial tension broke out within the county. Those on duty were scheduled in three eight-hour shifts for twenty-four-hour coverage of their posts.

General Francis Marshall was instructed before leaving Camp Zachary Taylor to arrest the ringleaders of the mob that had stormed the courthouse. It was a task that the military general could not accomplish. The mob was seemingly leaderless. No individual or core group of individuals was inciting the mob that had stormed the courthouse or those who rallied behind them. It was an organic movement that faded quickly and dispersed at the sight of the bayonets fixed at the ends of federal troops' rifles. The primary goal of the military presence, however, was to keep the peace and to protect certain assets. Specifically identified were the courthouse, the arsenal at the University of Kentucky, tobacco warehouses (especially because of earlier threats made against those owned by Sheriff Rodes), and residences of those local officials whose lives had been threatened by the mob.

Civil authorities were not entirely disbanded for long. This was accomplished by a separate proclamation ordered by General Marshall on the evening of February 9, in which he directed and empowered "civil and criminal authorities in this County and State to assume and administer their usual functions" subject to any instance in which the general assumed

Stoll Field near the University of Kentucky campus, where troops encamped while martial law was in effect. *University of Kentucky Libraries.*

jurisdiction. And so civil authorities continued to function under the supervision of General Marshall, who was named the military governor of Fayette County. The morning *Herald* proclaimed at the beginning of the first full day of martial law in Lexington that "business [was] to proceed as usual under Army rules." There would be, of course, a few obvious differences. And although both the newspapers and the military reports suggested that Monday's hysteria had subsided, the new rules "laid down by the Military Governor" would not be relaxed. Order was to be restored and maintained. Even so, because most in Lexington were willing to follow the law, there are few if any accounts of the military control being particularly onerous. Of course, the suspension of constitutional rights and basic civil liberties through the imposition of martial law still had a significant impact on the daily lives of Lexingtonians.

Citizens were subject to search by troops "at whatever times it is considered advisable." Those in the downtown area were required to present identification upon demand, and no persons were permitted to carry either firearms or ammunition.

"Move along" was likely a common order heard during the days of martial law in Lexington, as loitering, too, was prohibited. Those leaving the city limits were free to do so, but those entering or returning to the city could do so only with a pass.

Frank Carter, the owner of the Carter Supply Company on West Short Street, was issued a pass on February 10, 1920, to conduct certain work that would otherwise have been restricted. The pass was addressed as an "Order to Outpost" and signed under the command of General Marshall. It authorized Carter's business to "load and unload auto wagons in front of their place of business."

Taxis and trucks were requisitioned by the military forces in order to send out patrols for the Twenty-Sixth Infantry, which was assigned to outposts. The Twenty-Eighth Infantry largely took over the downtown area.

Governor Morrow continued to bring peace to Lexington as well. On the Thursday following the trial, he requested that the ministers in Lexington include in their sermons on Sunday a moment "devoted to the enforcement of law on the part of local officials and urging respect for and obedience to the law on the part of the people generally." Many ministers complied with the request. Several indicated that they had already planned such a sermon given the perceived need for such a message in the community.

According to reports, the citizens of Lexington did not show any antagonism toward the occupying federal troops and largely mourned for

A permit issued by command of General Marshall authorizing the Carter Supply Company to load and unload "auto wagons" during martial law. *J. Winston Coleman Scrapbook Collection, Transylvania University Library.*

what had taken place. By February 16, a full week after the February 9 riot, nearly all of the troops assigned to Lexington had returned to Camp Zachary Taylor. Among those returning was General Francis Marshall. In his stead, General Marshall designated Lieutenant Colonel George E. Maddox to remain as the military governor of Fayette County by virtue of his being the highest ranked officer remaining in the military zone. Under Lieutenant Colonel Maddox remained a total of seventy-one men, as follows: from the Twenty-Sixth Infantry, one officer and twenty-eight men; from the Twenty-Eighth Infantry, one officer and twenty-nine men; from the medical detachment, one officer and two men; and from the Motor Transportation Corps, nine men.

Upon his departure, General Marshall also penned a letter to the editors of the newspapers, praising the people of Fayette County, whom he found to be largely "American citizens who love and respect our flag." He also used the opportunity to support a national policy of maintaining a standing national army to protect American interests both domestically and abroad at a moment's notice. In his letter, he urged the people of Lexington to write their representatives in Congress to support such a regular army.

Intelligence reports in the days following the withdrawal of troops continued to show a peaceful atmosphere. In his report of February 19, Lieutenant Colonel Maddox, the military governor, offered his opinion that martial law had served its "full purpose and should be terminated." He suggested that the ongoing presence of soldiers on the streets of Lexington served only as a reminder to the citizens "of their shame and, in time, cannot but become a source of active irritation." His report the following day, however, indicated that both Judge Kerr and Judge Bullock desired that troops remain.

In reliance of Maddox's intelligence reports and recommendation, the commanding general of Camp Zachary Taylor, General Charles Summerall, notified civil authorities in Lexington that martial law would terminate on February 22 at 11:30 a.m. Summerall had visited Lexington in the early days of martial law, though reports attempted to indicate that the visit was not connected with the presence of the military occupation. Military intelligence reports relating to this affair concluded with the final troop movements: "the entire command entrained at 7:00 a.m. Feb. 22, 1920, and arrived at Camp Taylor" at 11:45 a.m.

Maddox issued a proclamation bringing martial law to an end as "law and order have been restored in the County of Fayette." In his proclamation as military general "commanding by the authority of the President of the United States" declared an end to martial law and directed and empowered "the civil authorities to resume and administer their usual function."

Martial law was over.

Removing Lockett from the Courthouse

Will Lockett had been sentenced to die at the state penitentiary in Eddyville, Kentucky, on March 11, 1920. A logistical hurdle existed, however. After the trial, Lockett remained inside a cell on the third floor of the Fayette County courthouse for more than a day while his transportation to Eddyville was arranged. Around 8:30 p.m. on the day following the trial, action was taken to move the condemned. Every effort was made to ensure that Lockett's departure from the courthouse was not publicly known until he was far from Lexington. Earlier in the evening, General Marshall had ordered both the telephone and telegraph companies to sever all communications extending a distance of one hundred miles from Lexington. Both companies strictly complied so that both incoming and outgoing telegraph and telephone lines were frozen, thus preventing any communication regarding the movement of the prisoner. By his order, these modes of communication were not restored until one minute after midnight.

At the command of the military governor, Sheriff Rodes and two deputies escorted Lockett from his cell. Lockett was described at the time as silent.

He was offered water but declined. "No," was the only word reported to have been spoken by Lockett during this transfer. Save that solitary word, Lockett was otherwise silent. He was then ushered down the stairs. The *Leader* reported that Lockett fixed his eyes straight ahead; the *Herald's* account provided that Lockett's head was bowed. At the front door of the courthouse, the entourage was met by a guard of some forty troops. Just like those troops who had entered Lexington a few days earlier, these soldiers had their bayonets fixed. Fortunately, the presence of martial law for just over twenty-four hours had rendered this precaution unnecessary. Marshall ordered his troops to part, allowing the civilian authorities to escort their prisoner to the awaiting special train.

Soldiers closed ranks around the prisoner and his three escorts as they all processed to the train that waited on the tracks at Water and Upper Streets. Few others were downtown on the quiet winter evening. The only sound that broke the "solemn silence" was the rhythmic pattern of marching soldiers. It took only two minutes for the procession to arrive at the troop train. It promptly left at 9:00 p.m. for the two-hundred-plus-mile journey to Eddyville. On it, Will Lockett was accompanied by the sheriff's deputies as well as some four hundred soldiers under the command of Colonel Charles A. Hunt of the Eighteenth Infantry. Sheriff Rodes did not travel to Eddyville and relied on his deputies to deliver the warrant calling for Lockett's execution to the warden of the penitentiary. Despite the silencing of all telephones and telegraphs, word spread within an hour or so of the train's departure that Lockett was no longer in Lexington.

When the train arrived in Eddyville, Lockett was turned over to the warden of the state penitentiary. Within thirty minutes, the four hundred troops who had accompanied him from Lexington took the same train back to Camp Taylor. The entire trip was "without incident."

AN INVESTIGATION

With Lockett out of Lexington, there was general hope and desire that Lexington would resume a sense of normalcy. Fayette County coroner John T. Anglin, whose signature can be found on the death certificates of Geneva Hardman as well as each of the riot victims, ordered an inquest to be conducted. The purpose of the inquest was to determine the cause of death for each of the riot victims in the collective, rather than to determine the cause of each individual death. Initially, the inquest was to occur on the Friday following the trial, but it was postponed to the following Monday. Witnesses for this inquest were summoned to the office of Magistrate Charles P. Dodd in the courthouse.

More significantly, General Marshall ordered that a grand jury be convened after conferring with a group of "prominent citizens" on February 12. This was two days after the trial and only a day after Lockett had been removed from Lexington. After this meeting, Marshall issued a proclamation ordering Judge Kerr of the Fayette Circuit Court to "impanel a special grand jury...to investigate the occurrence on Monday...and the actions of those who resisted the civil authorities." With the upcoming special grand jury, it was decided to keep the troops on guard "a few days longer" despite conditions in and around Lexington. Though the city was "nearly normal," extraordinary precaution was still being taken. Judge Kerr chose to have the grand jury meet first on Saturday, February 14. According to military intelligence reports, that day would be quiet—a descriptor that echoed the general tone of each of the days that had elapsed since the riotous events of February 9.

A jury commission quickly selected twenty-four names to serve in the jury pool. Those individuals, as identified by the newspapers, were real estate broker J. Bruce Davis, lumberman I. Newton Combs, druggist James B. Hall, merchant Harry S. Brewer, farmer Dan W. Scott, merchant Cal T. Russell, president of the Phoenix & Third National Bank William A. McDowell, vice president of the Security Trust Company R.T. Anderson, lumberman A.R. Stephens, capitalist R.R. Harting, tobacco dealer Esten Spears, tobacco farmer Samuel H. Halley, capitalist C.H. Berryman, wholesale grocer J. Clay Hunt, farmer Charles R. Thompson, tobacco farmer and horseman S.T. Harbison Sr., clothing merchant John G. Cox, salesman R.A. VanDervee and businessman and board of commerce president Frank B. Jones, capitalist Ernest B. Ellis, tobacco man and farmer William Preston, farmer Charles C. Patrick, construction engineer and farmer Silas Mason, and farmer and tobacco man James A. Hulett. Sheriff Rodes and his deputies quickly summoned each of the proposed jurors to the courthouse to appear on Saturday.

From this group of twenty-four, Judge Kerr selected twelve. The charge to the members of the grand jury was to investigate all of Monday's events and "to vindicate the innocent as well as fix blame on the guilty." The final jury consisted of John G. Cox, who would serve as foreman, and William

McDowell, William Preston, R.R. Harting, R.T. Anderson, James Hulett, Major Ernest B. Ellis, Charles R. Thompson, J. Clay Hunt, C.H. Berryman, James B. Hall, and Frank B. Jones. Much like the jury that had sentenced Lockett to the electric chair in Eddyville, the makeup of the grand jury was wholly male, white, and well connected.

After the jurors were sworn, the grand jury took the testimony of about twenty witnesses, though the exact number of summonses issued was not disclosed. County Attorney Hogan Yancey advised the members of the grand jury that "if a man leads a mob and a death results, that man is guilty of murder in the first degree." If no death results, a felony indictment and prison sentence should still be the result.

In his charge to the jury, Judge Kerr emphasized the importance of a grand jury's role in the judicial system, describing it as the "mainspring in the mechanism of the court." Yet, despite the important role of a grand jury, there apparently was not a sufficient amount of care that went into the selection of the jurors. A week after being sworn in, the first grand jury was dismissed from service. The members of this jury were improperly selected, and the validity of the grand jury was called into question.

Colonel Allen, the commonwealth's attorney, determined that there "may be doubt as to whether the Jury Commissioners may select a special grand jury." The three-member jury commission believed that they were acting properly when they created the jury pool, but this was not the opinion of Colonel Allen. Because this was a special grand jury, not a regular grand jury, he argued that the jury commission did not have authority to act. As a result, a second grand jury was impaneled. Each of twenty-four names was drawn by Judge Kerr as prescribed by statute, and summonses were again issued so that the potential jurors could appear. As was the case before, the pool of twenty-four would be reduced to twelve men to serve on the second grand jury.

The members of the second grand jury were Albert D. Gilbert, R.A. Goode, J.M. Yancey, C.D. Calloway, W.J. Geary, W.T. Barrizger, John H. Wilson Jr., J.N. Haggard, J.T. McCormick, J.W. Adams, J.P. Sullivan, and David Ades. Albert D. Gilbert, an insurance agent, served as foreman. Of the group, three were merchants, two were insurance agents, four were farmers, one was a wholesale grocer, one was a retired businessman and one was a salesman. And as with both the jury during Lockett's trial and the first grand jury, all were white.

At 9:00 a.m. on February 21, 1920, Judge Charles Kerr charged the second grand jury to enforce and uphold the laws. He explained to the jurors that they were each assuming a position of public trust through their service and urged their "integrity of action" in carrying out their duties.

The first grand jury had taken quickly to its work, and it was widely believed that several indictments would be returned within a week. Because of the violated technicality and the need to impanel a second grand jury, the timeline for indictments was extended to weeks or even a month before any indictments were expected to be issued.

Although martial law had been extended over Lexington to allow the first grand jury to conduct its work, the last of the federal troops departed the morning after the second grand jury was impaneled.

When the grand jury returned its report to Judge Kerr, it offered no indictments. In it, they recounted the "murder of the young girl" that "shocked the whole community." The grand jury's report recounted the large number of "justifiably angry and infuriated citizens" who formed a "dense mass of people, all of whom were greatly and wildly excited."

The grand jury report identified most of those in the assembly as being curious bystanders with "no intention of indulging in actual physical violence." The report pointed to a small number of "men, mostly from other counties other than Fayette" who instigated and were involved in the disruption. The grand jury even interviewed some who admitted to inciting the crowd; for these individuals, the grand jury would have issued indictments had the jury believed that doing so was in the best interests of the community.

But the grand jury did not believe that indictments would move Lexington toward healing. Rather, the issuance of indictments and prolonging the saga would only "aggravate an already tense situation, engender more passion and bitter feelings in the county and State and keep alive such as now exists." And so, no indictments were presented by the grand jury.

The grand jury also praised all those officials and soldiers for "not allowing threats, intimidation and force" to further extend Lexington into a state of lawlessness. But the grand jury's strongest praise was reserved for Tupper Hardman, the brother of young Geneva who had passionately urged peace on behalf of his bereaved family. "We especially desire to express our sincere admiration for the superb courage, manliness and good citizenship" of Mr. Hardman. The grand jury observed that if Tupper Hardman "could control his natural indignation, horror and desire for vengeance" in spite of his proximity in both "blood and affection" for the victim, then surely any who "did not even know the girl" could defer to a sensible call for justice under the law.

THE CONSTITUTIONALITY OF MARTIAL LAW

Martial law ended in Lexington on February 22, 1920. It would mark the last time in the years immediately following World War I that military involvement was required on U.S. soil to respond to what was deemed a racially motivated incident. The military's success in restoring order does not, nor should it, suggest that the end might justify the means.

Governor Morrow's request for federal troops followed a wartime policy still considered by some to be in effect following the Great War. Under this policy, the governor of a state could—upon declaring an emergency—request the presence of federal troops in their jurisdiction without the need for the request to be channeled through Washington, D.C. Morrow's request was made directly to General Leonard Wood, who then commanded the U.S. Army's Central Department in Chicago. General Wood accepted and responded to the request.

Along with Theodore Roosevelt, Wood had organized the voluntary cavalry regiment at the outbreak of the Spanish-American War known as the "Rough Riders." It was during that conflict's Battle of San Juan Hill that Wood was promoted to the rank of brigadier general. Wood also had political aspirations. The previous fall, Wood ordered troops to quell emergencies in Omaha, Nebraska (a race riot), and Gary, Indiana (a labor strike). As he would do a few months later in Lexington, Wood oversaw the introduction of martial law in these communities. As the "law and order" candidate, Wood was the frontrunner for the 1920 Republican nomination for president of the United States. At the convention held in Chicago in early June, just five months after the Lexington affair, Wood led during the first seven ballots. His support then began to slip away in favor of a consensus candidate. On the tenth ballot, Warren G. Harding became the Republican nominee.

Wood's response to requests for federal troops on domestic soil did ultimately bring peaceful outcomes in Omaha, Gary, and Lexington. But the actions were nonetheless unconstitutional. In 1997, the army's Center of Military History published a book on *The Role of Federal Military Forces in Domestic Disorders*. In profiling the response to Lexington's "racial disturbance," the authors wrote that General Marshall "greatly exceeded his authority." There was no grant of authority by the president, no regulations in effect, nor "statutory authorization whatsoever." Marshall "clearly violated the doctrine of *Ex Parte Milligan* set down in 1866" by the United States Supreme Court.

In that seminal ruling, the Supreme Court ruled that citizens could not be tried in military courts where civilian courts were still functioning. In this 5–4 decision, Justice David Davis wrote that "martial rule can never exist when the courts are open." The circumstances in *Milligan* arose during the Civil War, when *habeus corpus* was suspended in the United States by Congress in a law signed by President Lincoln in 1863. Lincoln had, in reality, already suspended *habeus corpus*; the 1863 law was simply Congress's blessing upon Lincoln's prior actions. *Habeus corpus* is the foundational legal principle that allows an imprisoned individual to bring an action ordering the jailer or prison warden (or whomever has custody of the inmate) to bring the individual to court for a hearing to determine if the detention is lawful. It is embedded in Article One of the Constitution: "the privilege of the writ of *habeus corpus* shall not be suspended, unless when in cases of rebellion or invasion the public safety may require it."

Wood and Marshall appeared to have acted unconstitutionally by ordering troops to Lexington and installing martial law, and thus suspending habeus corpus, without any specific approval.

Part Five

ELECTRICITY OF SUFFICIENT INTENSITY

A SENTENCE OF DEATH

The trial jury's sentencing of Lockett to death would be the first death sentence issued by a Fayette County jury that would send the defendant to the electric chair. All previous death penalty sentences were carried out via hanging in the jail yard of the Fayette County jail on Short Street.

The prior tradition of public hangings had been abandoned, however. A chosen few were permitted to attend an electrocution as authorized by statute. Others desired to be present but could not attend.

The heartfelt expressions from across the nation received by Geneva Hardman's mother were not the only responses from great distances that made their way to Kentucky. Ms. Connie Neathery of Ardmore, Oklahoma, telegrammed Judge Frank Bullock the following message: "What would be necessary for me to do to get to see Lockett electrocuted March 11? Where will it take place? Will come if can get in. Wire me if it would be possible for me to see him and who could give a permit. Wire collect."

According to the *Leader*, Judge Bullock did respond to Neathery's telegram, although the response must have been inadequate, as she soon sent another telegram requesting the same information.

Of course, any reply could have not satisfied Neathery's unique request. Kentucky statutes outline who may be present as witnesses to an execution. The list included the electrician and the warden of the penitentiary, as well as the warden's deputies and guards. Sheriff Rodes, as sheriff of the county where the sentence was handed down, could attend. Prison commissioners, a physician, and the penitentiary chaplain would attend. The condemned could select three other persons, plus a clergyman, of their choice to witness their execution. The statute also set a limited number of newspapermen who could attend.

This list was limited, as the statute concluded with the strict demand that "no other person shall be permitted to be present." Obviously, this list did not include a curious spirit from Oklahoma.

Following the trial, John H. Carter, as clerk of the Fayette Circuit Court, signed the court's directive that Lockett "be conveyed as expeditiously, privately, and safely as may be by the sheriff of Fayette County, to the state Penitentiary in the town of Eddyville, Kentucky." Before sunrise on March 11, 1920, Lockett was to be executed in the following manner: the warden "shall cause to pass through the body of said defendant, a current of electricity of sufficient intensity to cause death as quickly as possible, the application of which current shall be continued until the defendant is dead."

The execution date of March 11 was only thirty days after the trial. This was the minimum time required by law, which did allow for appeals to be filed.

Kentucky's Penal Institutions

Construction of the state penitentiary in Eddyville began in 1884. Since its construction, it has served as the state's maximum-security prison. Eddyville was a community along the Cumberland River, though much of old Eddyville now lies beneath the waters of Lake Barkley, which was created in the 1960s. Today, the massive stone penitentiary nicknamed "The Castle on the Cumberland" dominates the shoreline. The "foreboding" and "fortress-like" structure was completed in 1890. Several politicians opposed the establishment of this second penitentiary in western Kentucky, fearing it would remove political power from those who ran the Frankfort penitentiary.

The original state penitentiary was built in Frankfort in 1798. When Eddyville opened in the 1880s, it was a branch of the main Frankfort penitentiary. But in 1912, significant changes occurred. The year prior, the electric chair was installed in Eddyville. Also in that year, John B. Chilton was named the fourth warden for the Eddyville prison. It was a role in which he would serve until his death in 1929. Finally, 1912

Also known as the "Castle on the Cumberland," the Kentucky State Penitentiary in Eddyville was the site of Lockett's execution in March 1920. The maximum-security facility continues to house inmates today. *Kentucky Heritage Council.*

The entrance to the Kentucky State Reformatory, formerly the state penitentiary, as it appeared in 1935. The area regularly flooded, and the facility was replaced by a new state reformatory in LaGrange in 1939. *Capital City Museum, Frankfort, Kentucky.*

was the year in which the facility in Eddyville was named the State Penitentiary and the old penitentiary in Frankfort renamed the Kentucky State Reformatory.

It was at the State Reformatory in Frankfort where Lockett was held preceding the trial and the State Penitentiary in Eddyville where he was taken after the trial to await his execution.

LOCKETT IN EDDYVILLE

Governor Morrow had cautioned Warden Chilton to increase his forces around Lockett to keep him safe until the appointed hour on March 11. Morrow gave every indication that he would hold the warden personally responsible for the safety of this prisoner. Although there had been no sign of any concerning activity in or around the penitentiary, no precaution would be overlooked, especially given the widespread news coverage that followed the riot.

The special train carrying Lockett to the state penitentiary arrived at 8:00 a.m. Between the railway station and the prison, soldiers with fixed bayonets guarded the route.

Will Lockett's cell on death row was watched over by three soldiers sent by Governor Morrow. A manned machine gun was also set up at the penitentiary. Inside Lockett's cell, however, the condemned seemed "more easy" than he previously did according to the *Leader*. Lockett spent most of his day praying and reading the Bible.

PETRIE KIMBROUGH

On the road to Dixontown, Will Lockett had given the alias of Will Hamilton to Officer White and Dr. Collette. Now, confined to his cell, Lockett offered another name to the warden: Petrie Kimbrough.

What was his true identity?

There was a Petrie Kimbrough born in May 1888. At the age of twelve, Petrie resided at the Christian County, Kentucky home of his parents, Charles and Tina Lockett. Lockett's 1914 marriage announcement in a Lexington newspaper identifies his parents as Charles and Lena Lockett, and his 1917 draft card utilizes the birthday of January 15, 1887. It is possible that Will Lockett contrived the Kimbrough identity, though it is more widely accepted that the Lockett name was adopted by Kimbrough after he left his childhood home in Christian County, Kentucky. The *Danville Advocate-Messenger* attempted to clean up the discrepancies in Lockett/Kimbrough's identity in a column published on March 9, 1920. This was two days prior to Lockett's execution.

In the *Advocate-Messenger* article, the condemned Will Lockett confessed to Warden John Chilton that his true identity was Petrie Kimbrough. Lockett/Kimbrough desired to confess his crimes more completely in an attempt to "get right." This followed his baptism in a "bath-tub in the prison annex" by a minister from a black church in Eddyville.

According to the *Herald*, Lockett asked one of his guards if he could see Warden Chilton for the purposes of making a statement. The *Herald* reported that "he had killed all of his victims by choking them."

The *Encyclopedia of Modern Serial Killers* explains that Kimbrough abandoned his home and his birth name after assaulting a white woman in 1905 in Todd County, Kentucky. The *Advocate-Messenger* then identifies three additional murder victims to which Lockett confessed as having killed. Warden Chilton typed out Lockett's confession. Lockett then signed the confession, although a copy of this signed confession does not appear to exist. References to it are found only in secondary materials.

In the confession, the three identified victims in addition to Geneva Hardman were: "Mrs. George Rogers, 40 years old, of Carmi, Illinois, in 1912; Eliza Morman, mulatto negro woman, 25 years old, of Evansville, Ind., on December 19, 1917; [and] Sallie Anderson Kraft, 55 years old negro of near Camp Taylor, on February 19th, 1919."

Was Will Lockett a serial killer? The veracity of his statement during the trial concerning the death of his wife a month earlier suggests a degree of honesty on his part. Perhaps the answer to this question would be in the affirmative.

Some have pointedly discounted these additional confessions in an attempt to cast further doubt on Lockett's guilt. If doubt can be cast over the legitimacy of the confession, the same could be true of Lockett's initial confession as well as the investigation and trial.

This argument ignores the identities of the women named in the confession. The *Lexington Herald*'s March 9 edition did not identify the names of these victims; it only provided their race and gender. But the *Advocate-Messenger* did list the names based on the now lost-to-history typewritten confession. The specifics contained in the confession, as reported by the *Advocate-Messenger*, lend more credibility to Lockett's serial confession.

One of Lexington's newspapers indicated that these other murders were only casually investigated for their ties to Lockett. And, furthermore, any such investigation was given up as interest was lost in the whole affair. Just as the second grand jury decided to not issue any indictments, so, too, was there the desire to drop any investigation into Lockett's other alleged victims.

Presumably, the precise names given and facts surrounding the crimes may have been hazy to Lockett as he confessed to them at the state penitentiary. The *Herald* commented that Lockett was "not particularly clear on dates." But each of the crimes to which Lockett confessed does connect to an actual death.

Mrs. George Rogers was likely Clara Miller Rogers, though Clara's husband's name was William. In December 1912, Clara was attacked by a black man and died of her injuries the following spring.

Eliza Morman died on March 30, 1918, though Lockett seemed to place his crime the preceding December. Morman's death certificate showed that she died by natural causes. Did Lockett commit a crime against her three months before her death? Already ill, was her death not more thoroughly investigated?

The third victim's name was Sallie Anderson Kraft. Skeletal remains were found near Camp Zachary Taylor just outside of Louisville in July 1919 and identified as Sallie Kraft, "a negro woman who had been missing since last March" according to the Louisville *Courier-Journal*.

The existence of these three women's stories and deaths neither confirms Lockett's involvement in their deaths nor acquits him. Ultimately, one conviction was all that was necessary for Lockett to become the thirty-second person to be administered the death penalty via the electric chair since it was introduced at the Kentucky State Penitentiary in Eddyville in 1911.

On the reverse of the document signed by Fayette Circuit Court clerk John H. Carter was the confirmation by Warden John B. Chilton that the wishes of the jury had been carried out. Will Lockett (aka Will Hamilton, aka Petrie Kimbrough) had been executed at 4:32 a.m. on March 11, 1920. The execution occurred "by causing to pass through the body of the within named Will Lockett a current of electricity of sufficient intensity to cause death."

LYNCHING IN KENTUCKY

Between 1877 and 1950, the Equal Justice Initiative reports, 168 lynchings of people of color occurred within the Commonwealth of Kentucky. History professor John Dr. Wright Jr. has independently studied the crisis of lynching in Kentucky and believes that the number through the 1920s exceeded 200. He described lynching as "one of the most repulsive and barbaric" forms of mob violence in his 1986 article "Lexington's Suppression of the 1920 Will Lockett Lynch Mob."

The "mob mentality" that can lead to lynching was certainly present in the Lockett case. Even "solid citizen types" would fall to this mentality and support the illegal and most disturbing method of taking another human's life. The strength of the Ku Klux Klan, even among local law enforcement, led to a lack of consequence for those who participated in or led the killings.

The prevalence of the lynch mob in Kentucky and the tradition of local authorities looking blindly to the murders make it all the more significant that the mob seeking to take Lockett's life met the resistance of local authorities. Not only did they resist the mob, they also suppressed it. Just a few short decades earlier, on the same courthouse square where shots were fired by troops upon those with that mob mentality, slaves were traded in one of the most "notorious and seamy slave marts" in the South.

Governor Morrow's predecessor, to whom he had lost a close-fought election for governor in 1915, Augustus O. Stanley, confronted a lynch mob in Murray, Kentucky, in January 1917. Governor Stanley's stated goal was not to "snatch the accused from punishment but to save him from violence." Just as Governor Morrow did with Lockett, the aim of upholding justice was paramount.

In certain elements of Kentucky society, lynching was strongly and properly opposed. In 1919, Kentucky voters overwhelmingly supported a state constitutional amendment that would hold local authorities responsible if a lynch mob succeeded within their jurisdiction. Following the passage of the constitutional amendment, state legislators set to work on six new laws that would provide a framework. Although those bills were passed in early 1920, they would not become law until the middle of the year.

For those firmly in the antilynching camp, it was a positive time. The Lexington mob had been repelled, and new laws would soon be in effect. Yet only a few weeks after Lockett's life was temporarily preserved for the cause of justice, a black man accused of assaulting a young white girl was lynched in Paris, Kentucky. This was only twenty miles from Lexington.

In March 1921, only nine miles from Lexington, a lynch mob was successful in seizing Richard James from the county jail in Versailles, Woodford County, Kentucky. On the morning of March 13, James was hanged from a cottonwood tree near Midway, in Woodford County. The following day, Governor Morrow penned letters to the Woodford County attorney as well as the judge-executive demanding action under the new laws. To Judge-Executive Edward Mulcahy he wrote:

I cannot believe that forty or fifty men can come into a town; forcibly enter a jail and hang a prisoner without leaving traces behind them which, if followed, would lead to their identification. It is my judgment that [a] *Court of Inquiry should sit at once. Delay will only give those guilty a chance to cover their tracks; collect their forces and by various means evade detection. Delay in this matter can and will lead to nothing.*

Governor Morrow utilized the new antilynching laws to remove the jailer from office. He also considered removing the sheriff of Woodford County, describing the whole affair as an "outrage against law and order." Ultimately, the machinations of local politics prevailed over the antilynching statutes, as the jailer's wife assumed his role after being appointed to it by the county judge. To worsen the whole affair, the Court of Inquiry called failed to indict any individuals or even to issue a criticism of the lynching.

The last lynching in Kentucky occurred in 1934, when Rex Scott was hanged from a tree in a Knott County graveyard after having been dragged from the Perry County jail by "thirty or forty masked leaders of an armed mob of approximately 300 men," according to the *New York Times*. Multiple indictments followed, and the jailer was removed by Governor Ruby Laffoon. Unfortunately, each of the indictments, when brought to trial, resulted in an acquittal.

Author's Note
and Acknowledgements

The story of Geneva Hardman's murder and Will Lockett's trial is well known among those who spend time studying the rich history of Lexington, Kentucky. My first encounter with the story was a reference by John D. Wright Jr. in his book *Lexington: Heart of the Bluegrass*. During a law school clerkship, my mentor and I spent many lunch hours walking the historic streets of downtown Lexington, and he would recount historic vignettes from the city's history, including the unveiling of the now-relocated statue of John Hunt Morgan astride his horse, Black Bess (which remains among my favorite stories); the murder of Betty Gail Brown; and the Lockett trial. He showed me where the bullets had grazed the old courthouse. It was another example of how history can be tangible, and its stories are ripe to be told.

My true interest in Geneva Hardman's story, however, occurred upon reading my minister's book about the history of my church, South Elkhorn Christian Church (Disciples of Christ). It is the same church that the Hardman family attended. It is the same church where Geneva's funeral was held. My then-pastor's book, *An Ever Flowing Stream*, restated the paragraphs found in Wright's *Heart of the Bluegrass*. I felt that more of the story needed to be told.

More of the story has been told. J. Winston Coleman Jr.'s *Death at the Court-House* remains the best account of the mob action and the events leading up to it. It is a practical, twenty-eight-page read focusing on the mob's sentiment, but it ignores the emotions of a grieving family and community over the loss of a young child. It also does not prepare the modern reader for an understanding of the legal system in 1920, and it could not, because Miranda rights were not constitutionally mandated until fourteen years after Coleman published his pamphlet.

As the father of three children, my heart grieves for Emma. To lose a spouse in one decade and two children (one so unbelievably young) within the same year the next decade is grief unbearable. And yet, she persisted.

As for Will Lockett, we cannot truly know if he was or was not guilty. Much doubt has been cast on the due process afforded Lockett and whether the trial and punishment meted on him amounted to nothing more than a legal lynching. It has become popular to question his guilt based on modern jurisprudence. But our current interpretation of constitutional law was not available to defendants in 1920—especially for those defendants who were black and who stood accused of killing a young white girl. Were Lockett tried today for his crime, he almost certainly would be found not guilty based on the known evidence (and, based on the known evidence, no defense attorney would have allowed a confession). Or perhaps investigators would have gathered more evidence. With the benefit of modern science, DNA evidence would either incriminate or vindicate.

But Will Lockett stood accused in 1920, not in 2020. He confessed to the crime, although the confession was almost certainly coerced. Certain facts given out by local officials (such as the inaccurate identity of the mob leader who stormed the jail as Ollie Troutman or the misidentification of Judge Bullock as the one who started the volley of gunfire on the courthouse steps) cast doubt on other contemporaneous statements.

Too, it is important that we not fall into the trap of presentism. This can occur when we introduce our modern ideas and perspectives into our interpretations of the past. Our present, twenty-first-century understanding of civil rights and due process cannot be superimposed over the events of history.

"The arc of history is long, and it bends toward justice," is a paraphrase of a quote often attributed to Dr. Martin Luther King Jr. The quote was frequently used by President Obama. The lesson of justice to be recognized from the story of Geneva Hardman and Will Lockett is one in which a lynch mob was repelled.

Whether you believe Will Lockett was simply "legally lynched" in thirty days' time or not does not change the fact that he did receive a trial. We cannot forget the achievement that exists when the first lynch mob in the South is repelled by local and state authorities.

It is entirely another thing to be convinced that Will Lockett did in fact murder Geneva Hardman. Of this second question, I am not firmly committed to either answer.

Based on a historical interpretation of the evidence, I can accept the conclusion that Will Lockett murdered Geneva Hardman. I find damning the scent tracking by Captain Mullikin's bloodhounds for some seven miles across the day. It led to Will Lockett. I find this single piece of evidence compelling. The more I learned about Mullikin, about his hounds, and about the breed's abilities, the more compelling that evidence becomes. Am I certain? Of course not. Any theory is possible, but I find the conclusion that Will Lockett killed Geneva Hardman the most plausible.

Of course, it is entirely possible that Lockett was present at the wrong place at the wrong time and that the dogs just happened to pick up his scent. We will never know. What we do know is that Geneva Hardman was murdered. We know that Will Lockett was quickly the subject of the investigation, that he was tracked, that he confessed, that he was tried, and that he was convicted. Since he was first suspected, a mob tried to take his life. The only thing that stopped that mob were bullets fired by guardsmen who sought only to keep the peace. And then we know that Lexington spent two weeks under martial law, which was intended only to maintain the peace.

How I approached this book evolved as my research continued. And my words were revised as my approach evolved. There are a number of individuals to whom I must express my gratitude.

My first book, *Lost Lexington*, was dedicated to my wife. I continue to express gratitude for her acceptance of my evening "writing hours," and for the many miles she drove while I worked on this book.

I want to thank my History Press editors. My acquisitions editor, Chad Rhoad, pressed me forward to meet a deadline that I never should have set for myself. Rick Delaney served as the copy editor for this project, and he made this book a better product. My friend Jason Sloan was an unofficial copy editor whose assistance was invaluable.

Many hands assisted with my research. Those folks at the Kentucky State Archives who helped me obtain old court records. Multiple people in the Lexington Public Library's Kentucky Room, especially Wayne Johnson and J.P. Johnson, aided in my research. Bobbie Daugherty, a part-time deputy clerk in the Breckinridge County Clerk's Office, helped me scour through old records. (A side note: that county clerk's office has a trove of historical content, as it has wonderfully archived both official and unofficial records.)

A friend and former minister of my church, Jerry Shepherd, made a most meaningful introduction, without which I would not have had the energy or commitment to complete this project. That introduction was to Anne McGregor. Anne is Geneva's great-niece (she is the granddaughter of Tupper and Nora Hardman). I thoroughly enjoyed the opportunity to meet with both Anne and her niece, Nora Conner. These two women were instrumental in my learning an entirely untold element of these events. Meeting with each of them and learning their family's story inspired me to continue working on this project.

Others who also lent a hand include B.J. Gooch from Transylvania University's Special Collections, Jason Flahardy from the University of Kentucky Libraries, and local historians Foster Ockerman Jr. and William Ambrose.

A big thank-you also goes out to Officer Robert Terry of the Lexington Police Department. In addition to his law enforcement duties, he also serves as the police department's historian. His incredible research, and his willingness to share it with me, have been beyond helpful, especially as it relates to the identities of the jurors and the other victims of Will Lockett.

My sister, Kirsten, greatly aided in reviewing an early manuscript and reminded me that my writing style can be too lawyerly. Hopefully, I listened.

Selected Sources

Coleman, J. Winston, Jr. *Death at the Court-House.* Lexington, KY: Winburn Press, 1952.

Jillson, Willard Rouse. *Edwin P. Morrow—Kentuckian: A Contemporaneous Biographical Sketch.* Louisville, KY: C.T. Dearing Publishing, 1921.

Johnson, E. Polk. *A History of Kentucky and Kentuckians.* Chicago: Lewis Publishing, 1912.

Kleber, John E., ed. *The Kentucky Encyclopedia.* Lexington: University of Kentucky Press, 1992.

Lexington Herald. Archived at the Lexington Public Library.

Lexington Leader. Archived at the Lexington Public Library.

National Register of Historic Places. Selected entries.

Wright, John D., Jr. "Lexington's Suppression of the 1920 Will Lockett Lynch Mob." *The Register.* Frankfort: Kentucky Historical Society, 1986.

Index

W

Y

About the Author

P eter Brackney is an attorney who practices law in his adopted hometown of Lexington, Kentucky. He and his wife have three children as well as a redbone coonhound named Shelby. He is a double alumnus of the University of Kentucky and has served on the boards of different local history and historic preservation organizations. His first book, *Lost Lexington*, chronicled the backstories of Lexington's landmarks that have been lost to history. He has blogged since 2009 at www.thekaintuckeean.com.

Visit us at
www.historypress.com
······································